Betty Crocker

chicken
tonight

100 Recipes for the Way You Really Cook

BICENTENNIAL
1807
WILEY
2007
BICENTENNIAL

Wiley Publishing, Inc.

D0420111

Published by Wiley Publishing, Inc., Hoboken, NJ

For general information on our other products and services or to obtain technical support please contact our Customer Care Department within the U.S. at 800-762-2974, outside the U.S. at 317-572-3993 or fax 317-572-4002.

Wiley also publishes its books in a variety of electronic formats. Some content that appears in print may not be available in electronic books. For more information about Wiley products, visit our web site at www.wiley.com.

Library of Congress Cataloging-in-Publication Data:
Betty Crocker chicken tonight : 100 recipes for the way you really cook.
  p. cm.
 Includes index.
 ISBN 978-0-470-17351-0 (cloth)
 1. Cookery (Chicken) I. Crocker, Betty.
 TX750.5.C45B488 2007
 641.6'65—dc22

          2007013500

General Mills

Directors, Book and Online Publishing:
Maggie Gilbert and Lynn Vettel

Manager, Cookbook Publishing:
Lois Tlusty

Recipe Development and Testing:
Betty Crocker Kitchens

Photography and Food Styling: General Mills
Photography Studios and Image Library

Wiley Publishing, Inc.

Publisher: Natalie Chapman

Executive Editor: Anne Ficklen

Project Editor: Adam Kowit

Editor: Lauren Brown

Production Manager: Leslie Anglin

Cover Design: Paul Dinovo

Art Director: Tai Blanche

Layout: Indianapolis Composition Services

Manufacturing Manager: Kevin Watt

Manufactured in China
10 9 8 7 6 5 4 3 2

Wiley Anniversary Logo: Richard J. Pacifico
Cover photo: Caribbean Chicken Kabobs
(page 148)

Dear Friends,

We know you have them, in the freezer or in your fridge, the staple you've come to count on time and again—chicken breasts. And why shouldn't you? They are easy to cook, amazingly versatile, easy to buy and economical. What's not to like?

That's why we wanted to give you 100 great ideas for this poultry favorite—not only simple ways to cook them but also fun new ideas. Learn how to grill, broil, sauté or microwave a chicken breast just right, then throw into a salad, toss on pizza or tuck into a tasty sandwich.

Branch out with chapters on global food—maybe Chicken Satay with Peanut Sauce—or enjoy a new twist on an old favorite. Cornmeal Chicken with Fresh Peach Salsa anyone? Whatever your mood, you'll find what you want right here.

Banish the bland, the blah and ordinary. Make chicken tonight and make it fun!

Warmly,
Betty Crocker

contents

Cooking Chicken Breasts— Four Easy Ways

Chicken breasts have got to be one of the most accommodating foods to cook. You can sauté, broil, grill or even microwave them. The key to getting juicy, tender meat is not to overcook it.

Start with boneless skinless chicken breast halves, about $1/4$ pound each. (If you forget to thaw the chicken overnight in the fridge, microwave-defrost it following the manufacturer's instructions.) Rinse chicken in cold water, pat dry with paper towels (season with salt and pepper if you like) and you're ready to cook.

To Sauté:

1   Heat about 1 teaspoon vegetable oil in 8-inch skillet over medium heat 1 to 2 minutes. (If you're cooking 3 to 4 chicken breast halves, use a 10- or 12-inch skillet.)

2   Add the chicken and cook 8 to 10 minutes, turning once, until outside is golden brown and juice is no longer pink when thickest part is pierced with knife.

To Broil:

1   Position oven rack 4 to 6 inches below the broiler. Brush rack of broiler pan with vegetable oil or spray with cooking spray. Set oven to broil.

2   Place chicken breasts in broiler pan and broil 15 to 20 minutes, turning once, until juice is no longer pink when thickest part is pierced with knife.

To Grill:

1   Brush grill rack with vegetable oil, or spray with cooking spray. Prepare the grill for direct heat following manufacturer's instructions. Heat to medium (this will take about 40 minutes for charcoal or about 10 minutes for a gas grill).

2   Place chicken breasts on the grill 4 to 6 inches from heat and grill, uncovered, 15 to 20 minutes, until juice is no longer pink when thickest part is pierced with knife.

To Microwave:

1   Arrange chicken breasts in microwavable dish large enough to hold pieces in a single layer. Cover with plastic wrap, folding back one corner to vent.

2   Microwave on I ligh until juice is no longer pink when thickest part is pierced with knife (1½ pounds chicken will take 8 to 10 minutes). Rotate dish halfway through for even cooking.

Cubed Cooked Chicken

Many of the recipes in this book call for cubed cooked chicken. Follow any of the methods here for cooking chicken breasts (or buy precooked frozen breasts), then cut cooked meat roughly into ³/₄-inch cubes. One pound boneless skinless chicken breast yields about 2 cups cubed cooked chicken.

KICK UP THE FLAVOR

Add more flavor to chicken breasts by marinating them before cooking. See Flavor Boosters, pages 138–139, for information and recipe ideas, or use your favorite store bought marinades and rubs.

CRISP-COATED CHICKEN BREASTS

Adding a breading before cooking gives you chicken breasts that are crispy on the outside and moist and juicy inside. Brush uncooked chicken breasts with milk, buttermilk, Dijon mustard or mayonnaise, then roll in bread crumbs, cracker crumbs or flour before cooking.

Chicken Dishes on the Fly

Start with **4 boneless skinless chicken breast halves** and you can have a great tasting dish done in under 20 minutes. When time is of the essence, try these speedy recipes, or raid the refrigerator and see what inspires you.

Tip

For extra speedy, even cooking, pound chicken breasts to $1/4$-inch thickness between sheets of waxed paper, using a mallet, pounder or rolling pin.

Fresh Herb Chicken

Melt 1 tablespoon butter in 12-inch nonstick skillet over medium heat. Add chicken and brown on each side. Add $1/4$ cup dry white wine or chicken broth, 2 tablespoons chopped fresh basil, dill or chives and $1/4$ teaspoon salt. Cook about 8 minutes, turning once, or until chicken is no longer pink in center.

Pesto Chicken

Heat 1 tablespoon olive oil in 12-inch nonstick skillet over medium heat. Add chicken and cook about 10 minutes, turning once, until chicken is no longer pink in center. A few minutes before removing from heat, spoon 1 to 2 tablespoons purchased pesto over each piece and sprinkle with shredded mozzarella cheese; cover skillet to melt cheese.

Ranch Chicken

Heat 2 tablespoons oil in 12-inch nonstick skillet over medium heat. Dip chicken in $1/4$ cup ranch dressing, then coat with $1/3$ cup dry Italian-style or seasoned bread crumbs. Cook about 10 minutes, turning once, or until chicken is no longer pink in center.

Caesar Chicken

Heat $1/4$ cup Caesar dressing (not creamy type) in 12-inch nonstick skillet over medium heat. Add chicken and cook about 10 minutes, turning once, or until chicken is no longer pink in center. A few minutes before removing from heat, sprinkle chicken with 1 cut-up tomato and $1/2$ cup crumbled feta cheese; cover skillet to soften cheese.

Buffalo Chicken

Heat 1 tablespoon oil in 12-inch nonstick skillet over medium heat. Add chicken and brown on each side. Mix together 12 cups barbecue sauce and 1 teaspoon red pepper sauce. Pour over chicken, turning to coat. Cook about 8 minutes, turning once, or until chicken is no longer pink in center. A few minutes before removing from heat, sprinkle each chicken breast with about 2 teaspoons crumbled blue cheese; cover skillet to melt cheese.

Fajita Chicken

Heat 2 tablespoons oil in 12-inch nonstick skillet over medium heat. Coat chicken with an entire 1.27 ounce envelope dry fajita seasoning mix. Add chicken and cook about 8 minutes, turning once, or until chicken is no longer pink in center. During last 4 minutes of cooking, add 1 small bell pepper, cut into strips, and 1 medium onion, thinly sliced, stirring once or twice.

1

soups, stews, sandwiches and pizza

Italian Chicken Noodle Soup

Prep Time: 35 min ■ Start to Finish: 35 min ■ 6 Servings (1½ cups each)

1 tablespoon olive or vegetable oil
2 boneless skinless chicken breasts (about ½ lb), cut into ½-inch pieces
1 medium onion, chopped (½ cup)
2 cans (14 oz each) chicken broth
2 cups water
3 medium carrots, sliced (1½ cups)
2 cups broccoli florets
1½ cups uncooked medium egg noodles
1 teaspoon dried basil leaves
½ teaspoon garlic-pepper blend
¼ cup shredded Parmesan cheese

1 In 4-quart saucepan, heat oil over medium heat. Add chicken. Cook 4 to 6 minutes, stirring occasionally, until no longer pink in center. Stir in onion. Cook 2 to 3 minutes, stirring occasionally, until onion is tender.

2 Stir in broth, water and carrots. Heat to boiling. Cook 5 minutes over medium heat. Stir in broccoli, noodles, basil and garlic-pepper blend. Heat to boiling; reduce heat. Simmer uncovered 8 to 10 minutes, stirring occasionally, until vegetables and noodles are tender.

3 Top each serving with cheese.

Sweet, earthy parsnips are cousins to carrots, celery and parsley and they look like large white carrots. Give them a try!

1 Serving: Calories 170 (Calories from Fat 50); Total Fat 6g (Saturated Fat 2g); Cholesterol 35mg; Sodium 710mg; Total Carbohydrate 13g (Dietary Fiber 2g); Protein 15g

Chicken Pilaf Soup

Prep Time: 35 min ▪ Start to Finish: 35 min ▪ 4 Servings

2 cups broccoli flowerets
$1/4$ teaspoon ground cumin
$1/2$ lb boneless, skinless chicken breasts, cut into 1-inch cubes
2 cans (14 oz each) clear chicken broth
1 package (6.09 oz) rice pilaf mix

Mix all ingredients in 3-quart saucepan. Heat to boiling, stirring occasionally; reduce heat. Simmer uncovered about 25 minutes, stirring occasionally, until rice is tender.

1 Serving: Calories 170 (Calories from Fat 45); Total Fat 5g (Saturated Fat 1g); Cholesterol 30mg; Sodium 1010mg; Total Carbohydrate 14g (Dietary Fiber 2g); Protein 19g

Chicken-Broccoli-Tortellini Soup

Prep Time: 21 min ▪ Start to Finish: 21 min ▪ 4 Servings

1 tablespoon olive or vegetable oil
1 small onion, chopped ($\frac{1}{4}$ cup)
1 can (14 oz) chicken broth
$\frac{1}{2}$ cup water
$\frac{1}{2}$ teaspoon Italian seasoning
1 box (10 oz) frozen cut broccoli in cheese-flavored sauce
1 package (9 oz) refrigerated cheese-filled tortellini
1 cup cubed cooked chicken (about 8 oz)
1 large plum (Roma) tomato, chopped ($\frac{1}{2}$ cup)
$\frac{1}{4}$ cup shredded Parmesan cheese

1 In 2-quart saucepan, heat oil over medium-high heat. Add onion; cook about 2 minutes, stirring frequently, until crisp-tender.

2 Stir in broth, water, Italian seasoning, frozen broccoli in cheese sauce and tortellini. Heat to boiling, stirring occasionally and breaking up broccoli.

3 Stir in chicken. Cook about 4 minutes, stirring occasionally, until tortellini is tender. Stir in tomato. Top each serving with 1 tablespoon cheese.

1 Serving: Calories 320 (Calories from Fat 160); Total Fat 18g (Saturated Fat 7g); Cholesterol 100mg; Sodium 920mg; Total Carbohydrate 18g (Dietary Fiber 2g); Protein 24g

Chicken and Root Vegetable Soup

Prep Time: 45 min ▪ Start to Finish: 45 min ▪ 6 Servings

2 tablespoons butter or margarine
1 small onion, finely chopped ($^1/_4$ cup)
3 medium carrots, thinly sliced (1 cup)
3 medium parsnips, peeled and sliced (1 cup)
1 medium leek, sliced (2 cups)
7 cups chicken broth
1 cup uncooked orzo pasta (6 oz)
2 cups shredded cooked chicken breast (about 1 lb)
2 tablespoons chopped fresh or 2 teaspoons dried dill weed
$^1/_2$ teaspoon salt

1 Melt butter in Dutch oven over medium heat. Add onion, carrots, parsnips and leek and cook, stirring occasionally, until carrots are tender.

2 Stir in broth and pasta. Heat to boiling; reduce heat to low. Cover and simmer about 15 minutes, stirring occasionally, until pasta is tender.

3 Stir in remaining ingredients. Cover and simmer about 5 minutes or until hot.

1 Serving: Calories 285 (Calories from Fat 70); Total Fat 8g (Saturated Fat 2g); Cholesterol 40mg; Sodium 1520mg; Total Carbohydrate 34g (Dietary Fiber 5g); Protein 24g

Chicken and Vegetable Bow-Tie Soup

Prep Time: 30 min ■ Start to Finish: 30 min ■ 6 Servings

1 teaspoon oil
1 stalk celery, thinly sliced
3 (14 oz) cans chicken broth
2 cups water
1 (1-lb) package frozen broccoli, carrots and cauliflower
2 cups cubed cooked chicken (about 1 lb)
1 cup uncooked bow-tie pasta (farfalle)
¼ teaspoon poultry seasoning

1 Heat oil in large saucepan over medium high heat until hot. Add celery, cook and stir 2 to 3 minutes or until crisp-tender.

2 Add broth and water; bring to a boil. Add frozen vegetables; return to a boil.

3 Add all remaining ingredients; mix well. Simmer 15 minutes or until pasta and vegetables are tender, stirring occasionally. If desired, season to taste with salt and pepper.

1 Serving: Calories 180 (Calories from Fat 55); Total Fat 6g (Saturated Fat 1g); Cholesterol 40mg; Sodium 990mg; Total Carbohydrate 11g (Dietary Fiber 3g); Protein 20g

Asian Chicken Noodle Soup

Prep Time: 20 min ▪ Start to Finish: 20 min ▪ 4 Servings

3 cups water

1 package (3 oz) chicken-flavor ramen noodle soup mix

2 cups cut-up cooked chicken (about 1 lb)

2 medium stalks bok choy (with leaves), cut into ¼-inch slices

1 medium carrot, sliced (½ cup)

1 teaspoon sesame oil, if desired

1 Heat water to boiling in 3-quart saucepan. Break block of noodles; reserve seasoning packet. Stir noodles, chicken, bok choy and carrot into water. Heat to boiling; reduce heat to low. Simmer uncovered 3 minutes, stirring occasionally.

2 Stir in contents of seasoning packet and sesame oil.

If you wind up with more bok choy than you need, use the extra to make a simple side salad. Top with a few sliced radishes and a tangy vinaigrette dressing.

1 Serving: Calories 225 (Calories from Fat 80); Total Fat 9g (Saturated Fat 9g); Cholesterol 60mg; Sodium 420mg; Total Carbohydrate 14g (Dietary Fiber 1g); Protein 22g

Chicken Stew over Biscuits

Prep Time: 20 min ▪ Start to Finish: 20 min ▪ 4 Servings

1 tablespoon vegetable oil
$\frac{1}{2}$ teaspoon dried thyme leaves
$\frac{1}{4}$ teaspoon salt
$\frac{1}{4}$ teaspoon pepper
1 pound boneless skinless chicken breast halves, cut into 1-inch pieces
1 package (16 oz) frozen mixed vegetables
1 container (10 oz) refrigerated Alfredo sauce
$\frac{1}{2}$ teaspoon Dijon mustard
8 baking powder biscuits

1 Heat oil, thyme, salt and pepper in 10-inch nonstick skillet over medium-high heat. Cook chicken in oil mixture, stirring occasionally, until no longer pink in center.

2 Stir in remaining ingredients except biscuits; reduce heat to medium. Cover and cook 5 to 6 minutes, stirring occasionally, until hot.

3 Split open biscuits. Serve stew over biscuits.

1 Serving: Calories 835 (Calories from Fat 475); Total Fat 53g (Saturated Fat 19g); Cholesterol 115mg; Sodium 1290mg; Total Carbohydrate 59g (Dietary Fiber 7g); Protein 38g

Chicken-Garbanzo Paprika Stew

Prep Time: 1 hr ■ Start to Finish: 1 hr ■ 6 Servings

3 large onions, sliced
4 slices turkey bacon, finely chopped
2¹/₂ cups clear chicken broth
1 tablespoon cider vinegar
1 lb boneless skinless chicken breasts, cut into 1¹/₂-inch cubes
2 teaspoons paprika
1 cup tomato juice
1 tablespoon tomato paste
1 can (15 to 16 oz) garbanzo beans (chick peas), drained
1¹/₂ teaspoons chopped fresh or ¹/₂ teaspoon dried thyme leaves
¹/₄ teaspoon pepper
1 clove garlic, finely chopped
1 bay leaf
1 tablespoon cornstarch
1 tablespoon cold water
3 cups hot cooked couscous

1 Spray 12-inch skillet with nonstick cooking spray. Cook onions, bacon, ¹/₂ cup of the broth and the vinegar in skillet over medium heat about 10 minutes or until liquid has evaporated. Stir in chicken. Sprinkle with paprika. Cook 3 to 5 minutes, stirring occasionally, until chicken is brown on all sides.

2 Stir in remaining 2 cups broth, the tomato juice, tomato paste, beans, thyme, pepper, garlic and bay leaf. Heat to boiling; reduce heat. Cover and simmer about 30 minutes, stirring occasionally, to blend flavors.

3 Mix cornstarch and cold water; stir into stew. Cook about 3 minutes or until sauce thickens. Remove bay leaf. Serve over couscous.

1 Serving: Calories 485 (Calories from Fat 170); Total Fat 19g (Saturated Fat 7g); Cholesterol 95mg; Sodium 630mg; Total Carbohydrate 41g (Dietary Fiber 3g); Protein 38g

Harvest Chicken Stew

Prep Time: 15 min ▪ Start to Finish: 1 hr 25 min ▪ 6 Servings

4 cups 1-inch cubes peeled eggplant (about 1 lb)
4 cups ⅛-inch slices small red potatoes (about 8)
4 medium carrots, sliced
3 medium onions, cut into fourths
2 cans (14 oz each) clear chicken broth
⅔ cup chopped fresh parsley
2 tablespoons chopped fresh or 2 teaspoons dried thyme leaves
¼ teaspoon salt
¼ teaspoon pepper
½ cup cold water
2 tablespoons all-purpose flour
6 boneless skinless chicken breast halves (about 1½ lb), cut into fourths
¼ cup tomato paste
2 tablespoons lemon juice

1 Heat oven to 350°F. Mix eggplant, potatoes, carrots, onions, broth, parsley, thyme, salt and pepper in ovenproof Dutch oven. Cover and bake 50 minutes.

2 Shake cold water and flour in tightly covered container. Stir flour mixture and remaining ingredients into stew. Cover and bake about 20 minutes longer or until potatoes are tender and chicken is no longer pink in center.

1 Serving: Calories 340 (Calories from Fat 45); Total Fat 5g (Saturated Fat 1g); Cholesterol 60mg; Sodium 720mg; Total Carbohydrate 49g (Dietary Fiber 7g); Protein 32g

Mustardy Chicken and Dumplings

Prep Time: 15 min ■ Start to Finish: 35 min ■ 6 Servings

1 tablespoon vegetable oil
4 boneless skinless chicken breasts (about 1¼ lb), cut into bite-size pieces
1 medium onion, chopped (½ cup)
2 cups milk
2 cups frozen mixed vegetables
1 can (10¾ oz) condensed cream of chicken soup
1 tablespoon yellow mustard
1 ½ cups Original Bisquick® mix

1 In 4-quart Dutch oven, heat oil over medium-high heat. Add chicken and onion; cook 6 to 8 minutes, stirring occasionally, until chicken is no longer pink in center and onion is tender.

2 Stir in 1½ cups of the milk, the mixed vegetables, soup and mustard. Heat to boiling.

3 In small bowl, stir Bisquick mix and remaining ½ cup milk until soft dough forms. Drop dough by 6 spoonfuls onto chicken mixture; reduce heat to low. Cover; cook 20 minutes.

1 Serving: Calories 390 (Calories from Fat 130); Total Fat 15g (Saturated Fat 4g); Cholesterol 65mg; Sodium 930mg; Total Carbohydrate 36g (Dietary Fiber 3g); Protein 29g

Chicken Salad Pita Sandwiches

Prep Time: 15 min ■ Start to Finish: 45 min ■ 2 Sandwiches (2 halves each)

1 cup chopped cooked chicken breast (about 8 oz)
1/4 cup fat-free honey Dijon dressing
1/4 cup chopped cucumber
1/4 cup chopped tomato
1 tablespoon finely chopped cashews
2 whole wheat pita breads (6 inch), cut in half to form pockets
2 tablespoons fat-free mayonnaise or salad dressing

1 In small bowl, mix chicken, dressing, cucumber, tomato and cashews. Cover and refrigerate at least 30 minutes until chilled.

2 Just before serving, spread insides of pita pockets with mayonnaise. Fill pockets with chicken mixture.

Serve this healthy chicken salad on top of a lettuce leaf. Omit the mayonnaise, and serve pita wedges on the side.

1 Sandwich: Calories 360 (Calories from Fat 70); Total Fat 7g (Saturated Fat 2g); Cholesterol 60mg; Sodium 830mg; Total Carbohydrate 50g (Dietary Fiber 6g); Protein 28g

Chicken Salad Croissants

Prep Time: 15 min ▪ Start to Finish: 1 hr 25 min ▪ 2 Servings

2 boneless skinless chicken breast halves (¹/₂ lb)
¹/₄ cup creamy ranch dressing
¹/₂ teaspoon yellow mustard
¹/₄ cup chopped cucumber
¹/₄ cup chopped tomato
2 tablespoons chopped cashews
2 croissants, split
1 tablespoon butter, margarine, mayonnaise or salad dressing
Lettuce, if desired

1 Arrange chicken, thickest parts to outside edge, in 2-cup microwavable casserole or on microwavable plate. Cover tightly and microwave on High 3 to 4 minutes or until juice is no longer pink when centers of thickest pieces are cut. Uncover and refrigerate about 10 minutes or until cool enough to handle.

2 Cut chicken into ¹/₄-inch pieces. Toss chicken, dressing, mustard, cucumber, tomato and cashews. Cover and refrigerate about 1 hour or until chilled.

3 Just before serving, spread cut sides of croissant halves with butter. Spread chicken mixture over bottoms of croissants; top with lettuce and tops of croissants.

Feeling fruity? Skip the tomatoes and use mandarin orange segments or cut-up grapes instead.

1 Serving: Calories 640 (Calories from Fat 380); Total Fat 42g (Saturated Fat 16g); Cholesterol 160mg; Sodium 540mg; Total Carbohydrate 33g (Dietary Fiber 2g); Protein 34g

Curry Chicken Sandwiches

Prep Time: 20 min ▪ Start to Finish: 20 min ▪ 2 Servings

1 tablespoon butter or margarine, melted
1/4 teaspoon lemon pepper
2 boneless skinless chicken breast halves (1/2 lb)
Salt and pepper
1 tablespoon mayonnaise or salad dressing
1 tablespoon plain yogurt or sour cream
1/4 teaspoon curry powder
Lettuce leaves
2 kaiser or hamburger buns, split

1 Set oven control to broil. Mix butter and lemon pepper. Brush half of the butter mixture over chicken. Place chicken on rack in broiler pan.

2 Broil with tops 4 inches from heat about 4 minutes or until chicken just starts to brown. Sprinkle lightly with salt and pepper. Turn chicken; brush with remaining butter mixture. Broil about 5 minutes longer or until chicken is brown on outside and juices are no longer pink when center of thickest piece is cut.

3 While chicken is broiling, mix mayonnaise, yogurt and curry powder. Place lettuce on bottoms of rolls. Place chicken on lettuce. Top with dollop of mayonnaise mixture and tops of rolls.

Curry leave you cold? Then make an Italian sandwich by using 1/4 teaspoon dried basil leaves for the lemon pepper and 1/4 teaspoon basil for the curry powder.

1 Serving: Calories 385 (Calories from Fat 155); Total Fat 17g (Saturated Fat 6g); Cholesterol 95mg; Sodium 420mg; Total Carbohydrate 27g (Dietary Fiber 1g); Protein 32g

Cajun Chicken Sandwiches

Prep Time: 25 min ▪ Start to Finish: 25 min ▪ 4 Sandwiches

1 teaspoon fennel seed, crushed
1/2 teaspoon garlic salt
1/4 teaspoon white pepper
1/4 teaspoon ground red pepper (cayenne)
4 boneless skinless chicken breast halves (about 1 lb)
2 teaspoons vegetable oil
4 kaiser rolls, split
4 slices (1 oz each) Monterey Jack cheese with jalapeño peppers

1 Mix fennel, garlic salt, white pepper and red pepper. Rub chicken with fennel mixture.

2 Heat oil in 10-inch skillet over medium-high heat. Cook chicken in oil 15 to 20 minutes, turning once, until juice is no longer pink when centers of thickest pieces are cut. Place chicken on bottoms of rolls. Top with cheese and tops of rolls.

1 Serving: Calories 390 (Calories from Fat 135); Total Fat 15g (Saturated Fat 7g); Cholesterol 85mg; Sodium 660mg; Total Carbohydrate 30g (Dietary Fiber 1g); Protein 34g

Mix it up-try using Swiss or Monterey Jack cheese instead of the sharp Cheddar.

Grilled Chicken-Cheddar Sandwiches

Prep Time: 20 min ▪ Start to Finish: 35 min ▪ 4 Sandwiches

4 boneless skinless chicken breast halves (about 1¼ lb)

½ teaspoon seasoned salt

¼ teaspoon coarse pepper

1 medium Bermuda or other sweet onion, sliced

4 oz fresh mushrooms, cut in half (1½ cups)

1 tablespoon olive or vegetable oil

3 tablespoons creamy mustard-mayonnaise sauce

4 slices (⅔ oz each) sharp Cheddar cheese

4 slices sourdough bread

1 Heat coals or gas grill for direct heat. Flatten each chicken breast half to ¼-inch thickness between sheets of plastic wrap or waxed paper. Sprinkle with ¼ teaspoon of the seasoned salt and the pepper.

2 Mix onion, mushrooms, remaining ¼ teaspoon seasoned salt and the oil; toss to coat. Place in grill basket. Place chicken on grill next to grill basket. Cover and grill chicken and vegetables 4 to 6 inches from medium heat 10 to 15 minutes, occasionally turning and brushing chicken with 2 tablespoons of the mustard-mayonnaise sauce and shaking grill basket to mix vegetables. Grill until chicken is no longer pink when centers of thickest pieces are cut and vegetables are tender. Add bread slices to grill for last 4 minutes of cooking, turning once, until crisp.

3 Top each cooked chicken breast with onion-mushroom mixture and cheese slice. Cover grill until cheese is melted. Spread bread slices with remaining mustard-mayonnaise sauce. Top each bread slice with cheese-topped chicken breast.

1 Sandwich: Calories 380 (Calories from Fat 160); Total Fat 18g (Saturated Fat 7g); Cholesterol 100mg; Sodium 590mg; Total Carbohydrate 19g (Dietary Fiber 2g); Protein 35g

Caesar Chicken Paninis

Prep Time: 30 min ■ Start to Finish: 30 min ■ 4 Sandwiches

4 boneless skinless chicken breasts (about 1 1/4 lb)
4 hard rolls (about 5×3 inches), split
4 slices red onion
1 large tomato, sliced
1/3 cup Caesar dressing
1/4 cup shredded Parmesan cheese (1 oz)
4 leaves romaine lettuce

1 Flatten each chicken breast half to 1/4-inch thickness with meat mallet or rolling pin between sheets of plastic wrap or waxed paper.

2 Spray 8- or 10-inch skillet with cooking spray; heat over medium-high heat. Cook chicken in skillet 10 to 15 minutes, turning once, until chicken is no longer pink in center. Remove chicken from skillet; keep warm.

3 In skillet, place rolls, cut sides down. Cook over medium heat about 2 minutes or until toasted. Place chicken on bottom halves of rolls. Top with onion, tomato, dressing, cheese, lettuce and tops of rolls.

1 Sandwich: Calories 500 (Calories from Fat 180); Total Fat 20g (Saturated Fat 4.5g); Cholesterol 90mg; Sodium 750mg; Total Carbohydrate 37g (Dietary Fiber 3g); Protein 41g

Keep it easy and serve with raw baby carrots and red and green grapes.

Honey Mustard Grilled Chicken Sandwiches

Prep Time: 10 min ▪ Start to Finish: 30 min ▪ 4 Sandwiches

1/4 cup Dijon mustard
2 tablespoons honey
1 tablespoon chopped fresh or 1 teaspoon dried oregano leaves
1/8 to 1/4 teaspoon ground red pepper (cayenne)
4 boneless skinless chicken breast halves (about 1 1/4 lb)
4 whole-grain sandwich buns, split
4 slices tomato
Leaf lettuce

1 Heat coals or gas grill for direct heat.

2 In small bowl, mix mustard, honey, oregano and red pepper. Brush on chicken.

3 Cover and grill chicken over medium heat 15 to 20 minutes, brushing frequently with mustard mixture and turning once, until juice of chicken is no longer pink when centers of thickest pieces are cut. Discard any remaining mustard mixture.

4 Serve chicken on buns with tomato and lettuce.

Broil these sandwiches when you don't feel like firing up the grill. Just place the chicken on the rack of the broiler pan, and brush with mustard mixture. Broil 4 to 6 inches from heat for 15 to 20 minutes, turning once and brushing with additional mustard mixture.

1 Sandwich: Calories 270 (Calories from Fat 55); Total Fat 6g (Saturated Fat 1g); Cholesterol 75mg; Sodium 560mg; Total Carbohydrate 26g (Dietary Fiber 3g); Protein 31g

Chicken Fajita Wraps

Prep Time: 20 min ■ Start to Finish: 20 min ■ 4 Sandwiches

1 tablespoon chili powder
1 teaspoon salt
4 boneless skinless chicken breasts (about 1¼ lb), cut into thin strips
1 tablespoon vegetable oil
1 bag (1 lb) frozen broccoli, red peppers, onions and mushrooms
    (or other combination)
8 flour tortillas (8 inch)
Salsa, if desired

1 In large bowl, sprinkle chili powder and salt over chicken; toss.

2 In 12-inch skillet, heat oil over high heat. Cook chicken in oil 3 to 4 minutes, stirring frequently, until no longer pink in center. Stir in vegetables. Cook about 4 minutes, stirring frequently, until vegetables are crisp-tender.

3 Onto center of each tortilla, spoon about ½ cup of the chicken mixture. Fold top and bottom ends of each tortilla about 1 inch over filling; fold right and left sides over folded ends, overlapping. Serve with salsa.

Exercise your options! If you can't find the frozen veggie combo suggested, try a 1-pound bag of frozen corn, broccoli and sweet red peppers or any of your favorites.

1 Sandwich: Calories 520 (Calories from Fat 130); Total Fat 15g (Saturated Fat 3.5g); Cholesterol 85mg; Sodium 1370mg; Total Carbohydrate 56g (Dietary Fiber 5g); Protein 42g

Mou Shu Chicken Wraps

Prep Time: 12 min ▪ Start to Finish: 30 min ▪ 4 Servings

Plum Sauce

1 cup sliced plums

1/4 cup plum jam

1 tablespoon white vinegar

Wraps

1 tablespoon sesame or vegetable oil

1/2 lb cut-up boneless chicken
     breast for stir-fry

1/3 cup hoisin sauce

2 tablespoons grated gingerroot

3 tablespoons dry white wine

1 teaspoon sugar

3 cups shredded savoy cabbage

3 small carrots, shredded (1 cup)

8 flour tortillas (6 or 8 inch)

1 To make Plum Sauce, mix all ingredients in 1-quart saucepan. Cook over medium heat about 5 minutes, stirring occasionally, until plums are tender.

2 To make the wraps, heat oil in 10-inch skillet over medium-high heat. Cook chicken in oil 8 to 10 minutes, stirring occasionally, until no longer pink in center.

3 Stir in remaining ingredients except tortillas. Cook 4 to 6 minutes, stirring constantly, until cabbage is crisp-tender.

4 Warm tortillas. Place 1/3 cup chicken mixture on each tortilla; roll tortilla around filling. Serve with sauce.

Save some prep and cleanup time by using 3 cups coleslaw mix (8 ounces) instead of the savoy cabbage and carrots. Can't find fresh plums? Go ahead and use canned ones.

1 Serving: Calories 505 (Calories from Fat 110); Total Fat 12g (Saturated Fat 2g); Cholesterol 35mg; Sodium 820mg; Total Carbohydrate 83g (Dietary Fiber 7g); Protein 23g

Chicken French-Bread Pizza

Prep Time: 5 min ■ Start to Finish: 17 min ■ 6 Servings

1 loaf (1 lb) unsliced French bread
1 can (8 oz) pizza sauce
2 cups cubed cooked chicken (about 1 lb)
1 can (2¼ oz) sliced ripe olives, drained
1 cup shredded reduced-fat mozzarella cheese (4 oz)

1 Heat oven to 425°F. Split bread horizontally in half. Place bread, cut sides up, on cookie sheet.

2 Spread pizza sauce over bread. Top with chicken and olives. Sprinkle with cheese. Bake about 12 minutes or until cheese is melted and chicken is heated through.

1 Serving: Calories 305 (Calories from Fat 110); Total Fat 12g (Saturated Fat 5g); Cholesterol 60mg; Sodium 660mg; Total Carbohydrate 29g (Dietary Fiber 2g); Protein 22g

Double-Cheese, Spinach and Chicken Pizza

Prep Time: 5 min ■ Start to Finish: 15 min ■ 6 Servings

1 package (14 oz) prebaked original Italian pizza crust (12 inch)
1 cup shredded Havarti cheese (4 oz)
2 cups washed fresh baby spinach leaves (from 10-oz bag)
1 cup diced rotisserie or other cooked chicken (about 8 oz)
¼ cup chopped drained roasted red bell peppers (from 7-oz jar)
½ teaspoon garlic salt
1 cup shredded Cheddar cheese (4 oz)

1 Heat oven to 425°F. Place pizza crust on ungreased cookie sheet.

2 Top with Havarti cheese, spinach, chicken, bell peppers, garlic salt and Cheddar cheese.

3 Bake 8 to 10 minutes or until crust is golden brown.

1 Serving: Calories 380 (Calories from Fat 170); Total Fat 19g (Saturated Fat 11g); Cholesterol 70mg; Sodium 800mg; Total Carbohydrate 30g (Dietary Fiber 2g); Protein 23g

Why not buy bags of fresh spinach and shredded cheese? All the hard work is already done. By the way, you can use most any type of cheese in place of Havarti.

Chicken Gyro Pizza

Prep Time: 20 min ▪ Start to Finish: 45 min ▪ 6 Servings

2 cups Original Bisquick mix
1/4 teaspoon dried oregano leaves
1/2 cup cold water
6 slices chicken breast, cut into strips
1 can (2 1/4 oz) sliced ripe olives, drained
1/2 cup crumbled feta cheese (2 oz)
1 1/2 cups shredded mozzarella cheese (6 oz)
1 small tomato, chopped (1/2 cup)
1/2 cup chopped cucumber

1 Move oven rack to lowest position. Heat oven to 425°F. Spray 12-inch pizza pan with cooking spray. Stir Bisquick mix, oregano and water; beat vigorously with spoon 20 strokes until soft dough forms. Press dough in pizza pan, using fingers dipped in Bisquick mix; pinch edge to form 1/2-inch rim. Bake about 15 minutes or until golden brown.

2 Top crust with chicken and olives; sprinkle with feta and mozzarella cheeses.

3 Bake about 10 minutes or until cheese is melted. Sprinkle with tomato and cucumber.

1 Serving: Calories 300 (Calories from Fat 125); Total Fat 14g (Saturated Fat 6g); Cholesterol 30mg; Sodium 1140mg; Total Carbohydrate 28g (Dietary Fiber 1g); Protein 15g

2
satisfying salads

Quick Garden Chicken Salad

Prep Time: 25 min ■ Start to Finish: 25 min ■ 6 Servings

1 package (16 oz) fusilli (corkscrew) pasta
2 cups cubed cooked chicken (about 1 lb)
1 small cucumber, chopped (1 cup)
1 medium yellow or red bell pepper, chopped (1 cup)
1 large tomato, chopped (1 cup)
²/₃ cup spicy eight-vegetable juice
¹/₄ cup lemon juice
¹/₂ teaspoon freshly ground pepper
¹/₄ teaspoon salt
1 clove garlic, finely chopped

1 Cook pasta as directed on package; drain. Rinse with cold water; drain.

2 Mix pasta and remaining ingredients in large bowl. Serve immediately.

Using fresh lemon juice adds a special zip to this salad. It takes one lemon to get about 2 to 3 tablespoons of juice. To get the most juice out of a lemon, roll it firmly back and forth on the counter several times before juicing.

1 Serving: Calories 350 (Calories from Fat 35); Total Fat 4g (Saturated Fat 1g); Cholesterol 40mg; Sodium 240mg; Total Carbohydrate 57g (Dietary Fiber 2g); Protein 23g

Tropical Chicken Salad

Prep Time: 15 min ■ Start to Finish: 30 min ■ 2 Servings

2 snack cups (4 oz each) tropical fruit in lightly sweetened juice (from 16-oz package)
1 teaspoon grated lime peel
$1/4$ teaspoon salt
2 boneless skinless chicken breasts, cut into 1-inch pieces
$1/2$ medium red bell pepper, chopped ($1/2$ cup)
2 medium green onions, sliced (2 tablespoons)
1 tablespoon finely chopped fresh cilantro
1 bag (6 oz) fresh baby spinach leaves
1 tablespoon flaked coconut

1 Drain fruit cups, reserving juice. In small bowl, mix 2 tablespoons reserved juice, the lime peel and salt. Add chicken pieces; toss to coat. Cover; refrigerate 15 minutes, stirring once.

2 Meanwhile, in medium bowl, mix drained fruit, bell pepper, onions and cilantro; set aside.

3 Heat 10-inch nonstick skillet over medium-low heat. Add chicken with marinade. Cook 6 to 8 minutes, stirring frequently, until chicken is brown on outside and no longer pink in center.

4 In large bowl, toss spinach with remaining reserved juice. On 2 dinner plates, arrange spinach. Top with chicken and fruit mixture. Sprinkle with coconut.

1 Serving: Calories 310 (Calories from Fat 50); Total Fat 5g (Saturated Fat 2g); Cholesterol 75mg; Sodium 450mg; Total Carbohydrate 35g (Dietary Fiber 5g); Protein 31g

Greek Chicken Salad

Prep Time: 25 min ▪ Start to Finish: 25 min ▪ 4 Servings

Mint Vinaigrette

3 tablespoons lemon juice

1$1/2$ teaspoons chopped fresh or $1/2$ teaspoon dried mint leaves

$1/2$ teaspoon salt

$1/8$ teaspoon pepper

1 small clove garlic, finely chopped

Salad

6 cups bite-size pieces assorted salad greens

2 cups cut-up cooked chicken (about 1 lb)

$1/8$ cup crumbled feta cheese

1 medium tomato, cut into wedges

$1/2$ medium cucumber, cut lengthwise in half, seeded and cut into $1/4$-inch slices

1 small green bell pepper, coarsely chopped ($1/2$ cup)

4 medium green onions, sliced ($1/4$ cup)

12 Kalamata or large pitted ripe olives

1 To make vinaigrette, shake all ingredients in tightly covered container.

2 To make salad, toss vinaigrette and remaining ingredients in large glass or plastic bowl.

Try adding cut-up grilled chicken to this salad for a delicious char-broiled flavor. Or to save time, purchase cut-up grilled chicken from the refrigerated foods section of your supermarket.

1 Serving: Calories 195 (Calories from Fat 80); Total Fat 9g (Saturated Fat 3g); Cholesterol 65mg; Sodium 610mg; Total Carbohydrate 7g (Dietary Fiber 2g); Protein 23g

Cobb Salad

Prep Time: 1 hr 15 min ■ Start to Finish: 1 hr 15 min ■ 4 Servings

Lemon Vinaigrette
$1/2$ cup vegetable oil
$1/4$ cup lemon juice
1 tablespoon red wine vinegar
2 teaspoons sugar
$1/2$ teaspoon salt
$1/2$ teaspoon ground mustard
$1/2$ teaspoon Worcestershire sauce
$1/4$ teaspoon pepper
1 clove garlic, finely chopped

Salad
1 small head lettuce, finely shredded (6 cups)
2 cups cut-up cooked chicken (about 1 lb)
3 hard-cooked eggs, chopped
2 medium tomatoes, chopped ($1^{1}/_2$ cups)
1 ripe avocado, pitted, peeled and chopped
$1/4$ cup crumbled blue cheese (1 oz)
4 slices bacon, crisply cooked and crumbled

1 To make vinaigrette, shake all ingredients in tightly covered container. Refrigerate at least 1 hour to blend flavors.

2 Divide lettuce among 4 salad plates or shallow bowls. Arrange remaining ingredients in rows on lettuce. Serve with vinaigrette.

1 Serving: Calories 590 (Calories from Fat 440); Total Fat 49g (Saturated Fat 10g); Cholesterol 230mg; Sodium 640mg; Total Carbohydrate 12g (Dietary Fiber 4g); Protein 30g

Italian Chopped Salad

Prep Time: 20 min ■ Start to Finish: 20 min ■ 4 Servings

6 cups chopped romaine lettuce

1 cup fresh basil leaves

1 cup cut-up rotisserie or other cooked chicken (about 8 oz)

2 large tomatoes, chopped (2 cups)

2 medium cucumbers, chopped (1½ cups)

3 oz Italian salami, chopped

1 can (15 oz) cannellini beans, drained, rinsed

²/₃ cup red wine vinaigrette or Italian dressing

1 In large bowl, place all ingredients except dressing.

2 Pour dressing over salad; toss until coated.

1 Serving: Calories 500 (Calories from Fat 240); Total Fat 27g (Saturated Fat 4.5g); Cholesterol 55mg; Sodium 940mg; Total Carbohydrate 36g (Dietary Fiber 10g); Protein 27g

Light Lemon Dijon Chicken Salad

Prep Time: 20 min ■ Start to Finish: 20 min ■ 4 Servings

Lemon Dijon Dressing

$1/4$ cup reduced-fat mayonnaise or salad dressing

2 tablespoons lemon juice

2 teaspoons Dijon mustard

1 clove garlic, finely chopped

Chicken Salad

4 cups shredded romaine

2 cups shredded cooked chicken breast (about 1 lb)

$1/4$ cup sliced, drained oil-packed sun-dried tomatoes

1 hard-cooked egg, chopped

2 medium green onions, sliced (2 tablespoons)

$1/4$ cup shredded Parmesan cheese, if desired

1 In small bowl, beat all dressing ingredients with wire whisk.

2 Arrange romaine, chicken, tomatoes and egg on individual serving plates. Spoon dressing over top. Sprinkle with onions and cheese.

1 Serving: Calories 160 (Calories from Fat 80); Total Fat 9g (Saturated Fat 2g); Cholesterol 90mg; Sodium 220mg; Total Carbohydrate 5g (Dietary Fiber 1g); Protein 16g

Mediterranean Chicken Salad

Prep Time: 10 min ■ Start to Finish: 10 min ■ 6 Servings

2 cups diced cooked chicken (about 1 lb)
1 bag (10 oz) ready-to-eat Italian-blend salad greens
1 can (14 oz) artichoke hearts, drained and chopped
1 can (4¼ oz) chopped ripe olives, drained
¼ cup tomato-and-herb Italian dressing

1 Mix all ingredients except dressing in large bowl.

2 Add dressing; toss until coated.

Top it your way—try zesty Italian, Parmesan ranch, red wine
   vinaigrette or garlic ranch

1 Serving: Calories 195 (Calories from Fat 110); Total Fat 12g (Saturated Fat 2g); Cholesterol 40mg;
Sodium 500mg; Total Carbohydrate 11g (Dietary Fiber 5g); Protein 16g

Mandarin Chicken Salad

Prep Time: 20 min ▪ Start to Finish: 20 min ▪ 6 Servings

2 tablespoons butter or margarine
1 package (3 oz) Oriental-flavor ramen noodle soup mix
2 tablespoons sesame seed
$1/4$ cup sugar
$1/4$ cup white vinegar
1 tablespoon sesame or vegetable oil
$1/2$ teaspoon pepper
2 cups cut-up cooked chicken (about 1 lb)
$1/4$ cup dry-roasted peanuts, if desired
4 medium green onions, sliced ($1/4$ cup)
1 bag (16 oz) coleslaw mix (shredded cabbage and carrots)
1 can (11 oz) mandarin orange segments, drained

1 In 10-inch skillet, melt butter over medium heat. Stir in seasoning packet from soup mix. Break block of noodles into bite-size pieces over skillet; stir into butter mixture.

2 Cook noodles 2 minutes, stirring occasionally. Stir in sesame seed. Cook about 2 minutes longer, stirring occasionally, until noodles are golden brown; remove from heat.

3 In large bowl, mix sugar, vinegar, oil and pepper. Add noodle mixture and remaining ingredients; toss.

1 Serving: Calories 300 (Calories from Fat 130); Total Fat 14g (Saturated Fat 4.5g); Cholesterol 50mg; Sodium 330mg; Total Carbohydrate 28g (Dietary Fiber 4g); Protein 17g

Chicken Slaw Salad

Prep Time: 20 min ▪ Start to Finish: 20 min ▪ 4 Servings

2 cups chopped cooked chicken (about 1 lb)
2 cups shredded green cabbage
2 cups shredded red cabbage
1 cup shredded carrot (1 large)
1/4 cup sunflower nuts
1/2 cup low-fat Asian sesame-ginger dressing
1/2 cup chow mein noodles

1 In large bowl, place all ingredients except dressing and noodles.

2 Pour dressing over salad; toss to coat. Garnish with noodles.

1 Serving: Calories 280 (Calories from Fat 100); Total Fat 11g (Saturated Fat 2g); Cholesterol 60mg; Sodium 400mg; Total Carbohydrate 21g (Dietary Fiber 4g); Protein 23g

Chopped Chicken Asian Salad with Lime Dressing

Prep Time: 30 min ■ Start to Finish: 30 min ■ 4 Servings

Lime Dressing
$1/3$ cup frozen (thawed) limeade
$1/4$ cup vegetable oil
1 tablespoon rice or white vinegar
1 teaspoon grated gingerroot
$1/4$ teaspoon salt

Salad
2 cups chopped escarole
1 cup chopped cooked chicken (about 8 oz)
1 small jicama, peeled and chopped (1 cup)
1 large papaya, peeled and chopped (1 cup)
1 medium yellow or red bell pepper, chopped (1 cup)
$1/2$ cup dry-roasted peanuts
$1/4$ cup chopped cilantro

1 To make dressing, shake all ingredients in tightly covered container.

2 To make salad, place remaining ingredients except peanuts and cilantro in large bowl. Pour dressing over salad; toss until coated. Top with peanuts and cilantro.

1 Serving: Calories 425 (Calories from Fat 252); Total Fat 28g (Saturated Fat 5g); Cholesterol 30mg; Sodium 260mg; Total Carbohydrate 36g (Dietary Fiber 9g); Protein 16g

Wrap and roll! This cute finger food is fresh and crunchy—it's also perfect for your pals who are avoiding bread.

Asian Chicken Salad Lettuce Cups

Prep Time: 15 min ▪ Start to Finish: 15 min ▪ 24 Servings

2 cups finely chopped cooked chicken (about 1 lb)
4 medium green onions, diagonally sliced (1/4 cup)
1 can (8 oz) sliced water chestnuts, drained, finely chopped
1/2 cup spicy peanut sauce (from 7-oz bottle)
1 tablespoon chopped fresh mint leaves
1/4 teaspoon crushed red pepper flakes
24 small (about 3-inch) Bibb lettuce leaves (about 1 1/2 heads), breaking larger leaves into smaller size
1/3 cup chopped roasted salted peanuts

1 In medium bowl, mix all ingredients except lettuce and peanuts.

2 Spoon about 2 tablespoons chicken mixture onto each lettuce leaf. Sprinkle with peanuts.

1 Serving: Calories 60 (Calories from Fat 35); Total Fat 3.5g (Saturated Fat 0.5g); Cholesterol 10mg; Sodium 35mg; Total Carbohydrate 2g (Dietary Fiber 0g); Protein 5g

Stir-Fried Thai Chicken Salad

Prep Time: 30 min ■ Start to Finish: 30 min ■ 4 Servings

Sweet-and-Sour Dressing

1/4 cup vegetable oil

2 tablespoons sugar

2 tablespoons white vinegar

1/4 teaspoon salt

1/8 teaspoon crushed red pepper flakes

Chicken Salad

2 teaspoons vegetable oil

1 lb cut-up boneless chicken breast for stir-fry

1 medium zucchini, cut into julienne strips (2 cups)

1 1/2 medium carrots, shredded (1 cup)

6 to 8 green onions, cut into 1-inch julienne strips (1/2 cup)

1/4 teaspoon crushed red pepper flakes

4 cups chopped bok choy (stems and leaves)

1/4 cup dry-roasted peanuts

2 tablespoons chopped fresh cilantro

1 Mix all dressing ingredients.

2 In 12-inch skillet or wok, heat oil over medium-high heat. Add chicken; cook and stir about 5 minutes or until no longer pink in center.

3 Add zucchini, carrots, onions and pepper flakes; cook and stir about 4 minutes or until vegetables are crisp-tender. Stir in dressing. Cook and stir 1 minute. Serve over bok choy. Top with peanuts and cilantro.

Feel free to use an equal amount of spinach or green cabbage instead of the bok choy.

1 Serving: Calories 335 (Calories from Fat 205); Total Fat 23g (Saturated Fat 4g); Cholesterol 50mg; Sodium 290mg; Total Carbohydrate 15g (Dietary Fiber 3g); Protein 23g

Black Bean–Chicken Salad with Creamy Cilantro Pesto Dressing

Prep Time: 15 min ▪ Start to Finish: 30 min ▪ 6 Servings

Dressing

1½ cups lightly packed cilantro sprigs
½ cup shredded Parmesan cheese
⅓ cup pine nuts
⅓ cup olive or vegetable oil
¼ cup whipping cream
1 teaspoon grated lemon peel
1 tablespoon lemon juice
⅛ teaspoon ground red pepper
    (cayenne)
2 cloves garlic

Salad

2 teaspoons olive or vegetable oil
1 lb boneless skinless chicken breast
    halves, cut into ½-inch strips
1 teaspoon chili powder
¼ teaspoon garlic salt
2 cups uncooked rigatoni pasta
    (6 oz)
1 large tomato, chopped (1 cup)
1 can (15 oz) black beans
    rinsed and drained

1 To make dressing, place all ingredients in food processor or blender. Cover and process on medium speed until smooth.

2 To make the salad, heat oil in 10-inch skillet over medium-high heat. Cook chicken in oil 6 to 8 minutes, stirring occasionally, until no longer pink in center. Toss chicken, chili powder and garlic salt; set aside.

3 Cook and drain pasta as directed on package. Rinse with cold water; drain. Mix pasta, chicken, dressing, tomato and beans.

No fresh cilantro in sight? One container (7 ounces) refrigerated basil pesto can be used in place of the cilantro, Parmesan cheese, pine nuts and garlic.

1 Serving: Calories 550 (Calories from Fat 245); Total Fat 27g (Saturated Fat 7g); Cholesterol 60mg; Sodium 500mg; Total Carbohydrate 52g (Dietary Fiber 7g); Protein 32g

Chicken and Wild Rice Salad with Dried Cherries

Prep Time: 25 min ▪ Start to Finish: 25 min ▪ 6 Servings

1 package (6.2 oz) fast-cooking long-grain and wild rice mix
1 cup diced cooked chicken (about 8 oz)
1 medium unpeeled eating apple, chopped (1 cup)
1 medium green bell pepper, chopped (1 cup)
1 medium stalk celery, chopped ($\frac{1}{2}$ cup)
$\frac{1}{3}$ cup dried cherries, chopped
2 tablespoons reduced-sodium soy sauce
2 tablespoons water
2 teaspoons sugar
2 teaspoons cider vinegar
$\frac{1}{3}$ cup dry-roasted peanuts

1 Cook rice mix as directed on package, except omit butter. Spread rice evenly in thin layer on large cookie sheet. Let stand 10 minutes, stirring occasionally, until cool.

2 Mix chicken, apple, bell pepper, celery and cherries in large bowl.

3 Mix soy sauce, water, sugar and vinegar in small bowl until sugar is dissolved. Add rice and soy sauce mixture to apple mixture. Gently toss until coated. Add peanuts; gently toss.

Take this up a notch—add $\frac{1}{2}$ cup chopped dried apricots and sprinkle with $\frac{1}{4}$ teaspoon crushed red pepper.

1 Serving: Calories 130 (Calories from Fat 35); Total Fat 4g (Saturated Fat 1g); Cholesterol 0mg; Sodium 220mg; Total Carbohydrate 22g (Dietary Fiber 2g); Protein 4g

Chicken-Curry-Couscous Salad

Prep Time: 25 min ■ Start to Finish: 1 hr 25 min ■ 4 Servings

Curry Dressing
$1/3$ cup light olive or vegetable oil

1 tablespoon lemon juice

1 teaspoon sugar

$1/2$ teaspoon curry powder

$1/4$ teaspoon salt

$1/8$ teaspoon ground allspice

Salad
2 cups cooked couscous

1 cup diced cooked chicken (about 8 oz)

1 cup raisins

1 medium red or yellow bell pepper, cut into thin strips

6 medium green onions, chopped (6 tablespoons)

1 can (15 to 16 oz) garbanzo beans, rinsed and drained

$1/2$ cup chopped roasted almonds

1 To make dressing, shake all ingredients in tightly covered container.

2 To make salad, place remaining ingredients except almonds in large bowl. Pour dressing over salad; toss until coated. Cover and refrigerate about 1 hour or until chilled. Top with almonds.

This salad just begs for flatbread or pita breads to
    scoop it up.

1 Serving: Calories 710 (Calories from Fat 295); Total Fat 33g (Saturated Fat 4g); Cholesterol 30mg; Sodium 540mg; Total Carbohydrate 89g (Dietary Fiber 14g); Protein 28g

Pasta-Chicken Salad on Watermelon Wedges

Prep Time: 15 min ▪ Start to Finish: 15 min ▪ 6 Servings

1$^1/_2$ cups uncooked mini penne pasta or other small pasta (about 6 oz)
2 cups cut-up cooked chicken breast (about 1 lb)
1 cup red grapes, cut in half
8 medium green onions, sliced ($^1/_2$ cup)
$^3/_4$ cup reduced-calorie mayonnaise or salad dressing
3 tablespoons fat-free (skim) milk
1 tablespoon Dijon mustard
$^1/_2$ teaspoon salt
18 watermelon wedges, 1 inch thick
$^1/_4$ cup sliced almonds, toasted

1 Cook and drain pasta as directed on package. Rinse with cold water; drain.

2 In large bowl, mix pasta, chicken, grapes and onions. In small bowl, mix mayonnaise, milk, mustard and salt; stir into pasta mixture.

3 To serve, place 2 watermelon wedges on each of 6 dinner plates. Divide salad evenly among watermelon wedges. Sprinkle with almonds.

1 Serving: Calories 520 (Calories from Fat 150); Total Fat 17g (Saturated Fat 2.5g); Cholesterol 50mg; Sodium 620mg; Total Carbohydrate 72g (Dietary Fiber 5g); Protein 23g

Chicken-Thyme Pasta Salad

Prep Time: 25 min ■ Start to Finish: 4 hrs 25 min ■ 8 Servings

3 cups uncooked penne pasta (10 oz)
4 cups cubed cooked chicken
    (about 2 lb)
2 cups red grapes, cut in half
2 medium stalks celery, sliced (²/₃ cup)
¹/₃ cup chopped onion
3 tablespoons olive or vegetable oil
2 tablespoons chopped fresh or
    2 teaspoons dried thyme leaves,
    crumbled

1¹/₄ cups mayonnaise or salad
    dressing
1 tablespoon milk
1 tablespoon honey
1 tablespoon coarse-ground mustard
1 teaspoon salt
1 cup chopped walnuts, toasted

1 Cook and drain pasta as directed on package. Rinse with cold water; drain.

2 In very large (4-quart) bowl, mix pasta, chicken, grapes, celery and onion. In small bowl, mix oil and 1 tablespoon of the fresh thyme (or 1 teaspoon of the dried thyme). Pour oil mixture over chicken mixture; toss to coat.

3 In small bowl, mix mayonnaise, milk, honey, mustard, salt and remaining thyme. Cover chicken mixture and mayonnaise mixture separately and refrigerate at least 4 hours but no longer than 24 hours.

4 Up to 2 hours before serving, toss chicken mixture and mayonnaise mixture. Cover and refrigerate until serving. Just before serving, stir in ³/₄ cup of the walnuts. Sprinkle salad with remaining walnuts.

Don't be a chicken about math! About 2 pounds of uncooked boneless skinless chicken breasts equals 4 cups cubed cooked chicken.

1 Serving: Calories 690 (Calories from Fat 410); Total Fat 46g (Saturated Fat 7g); Cholesterol 80mg; Sodium 600mg; Total Carbohydrate 41g (Dietary Fiber 4g); Protein 29g

Hot Chicken Salad with Sage Biscuits

Prep Time: 20 min ▪ Start to Finish: 40 min ▪ 6 Servings

1/4 cup mayonnaise or salad dressing
2 tablespoons Original Bisquick mix
2 cups cut-up cooked chicken (about 1 lb)
1/4 cup shredded Cheddar cheese (1 oz)
2 medium stalks celery, sliced (1 cup)
2 medium green onions, sliced (2 tablespoons)
2 1/4 cups Original Bisquick mix
2/3 cup milk
1/2 teaspoon dried sage leaves

1 Heat oven to 425°F. Mix mayonnaise and 2 tablespoons Bisquick mix in medium bowl until well blended. Stir in chicken, cheese, celery and onions; set aside.

2 Mix remaining ingredients just until soft dough forms. Place on surface sprinkled with Bisquick mix; roll in Bisquick mix to coat. Shape into a ball; knead 10 times. Roll dough 1/2 inch thick. Cut with 1 1/2-inch round cutter dipped in Bisquick mix. Place close together around edge of ungreased 2-quart casserole.

3 Spoon chicken mixture into mound in center of biscuits. Bake uncovered 18 to 20 minutes or until biscuits are golden brown and chicken mixture is hot.

For a special touch, sprinkle this warm salad with
toasted sliced almonds and dried cranberries,
and garnish with fresh sage leaves.

1 Serving: Calories 370 (Calories from Fat 170); Total Fat 19g (Saturated Fat 5g); Cholesterol 50mg; Sodium 830mg; Total Carbohydrate 32g (Dietary Fiber 1g); Protein 19g

Asiago Chicken and Cavatappi

Caesar Chicken with Orzo

Chicken Carbonara Deluxe

Roasted Vegetable and Chicken Manicotti

Mexican Chicken–Sour Cream Lasagna

Asian Chicken and Noodles

Citrus-Ginger Chicken

Grilled Chicken with Chipotle-Peach Glaze

Cornmeal Chicken with Fresh Peach Salsa

Chicken Breasts Florentine

Tarragon Chicken and Leeks

Chicken in Fresh Herbs

Chicken-Rice Skillet

Layered Chicken–Black Bean Enchiladas

Sweet and Spicy Chicken Fajitas

Zesty Roasted Chicken and Potatoes

Spicy Southwest Chicken Kabobs

Chicken with Apricots, Brown Rice and Barley

Chicken and Rice with Autumn Vegetables

3

new twists on classics

Asiago Chicken and Cavatappi

Prep Time: 15 min ■ Start to Finish: 30 min ■ 4 Servings

1½ cups uncooked cavatappi pasta (5 oz)

⅔ cup boiling water

½ cup julienne strips sun-dried tomatoes (not oil-packed)

1 lb boneless skinless chicken breasts, cut into ½-inch pieces

¼ teaspoon garlic pepper

¼ teaspoon salt

2 cups frozen baby bean and carrot blend (from 1-lb bag)

¼ cup chopped fresh parsley

¼ cup shredded Asiago cheese (1 oz)

1 Cook and drain pasta as directed on package. Meanwhile, pour boiling water over tomatoes; let stand 10 minutes.

2 Meanwhile, spray 12-inch nonstick skillet with cooking spray; heat over medium heat. Cook chicken, garlic pepper and salt in skillet 2 to 3 minutes, stirring constantly, until chicken is brown. Stir in tomato mixture and vegetables. Cover and cook about 5 minutes, stirring occasionally, until chicken is no longer pink in center and vegetables are crisp-tender.

3 Stir in pasta; cook and stir until thoroughly heated. Stir in parsley. Sprinkle with cheese.

It's a 30-minute weeknight meal! If you like, substitute Parmesan cheese for the Asiago.

1 Serving: Calories 250 (Calories from Fat 55); Total Fat 6g (Saturated Fat 2g); Cholesterol 70mg; Sodium 620mg; Total Carbohydrate 22g (Dietary Fiber 4g); Protein 31g

Caesar Chicken with Orzo

Prep Time: 30 min ▪ Start to Finish: 30 min ▪ 2 Servings

1 teaspoon canola oil
2 boneless skinless chicken breasts
1 cup reduced-sodium chicken broth
½ cup water
½ cup uncooked orzo pasta
½ bag (1-lb size) frozen broccoli cuts
½ medium red bell pepper, cut into strips
2 teaspoons reduced-fat Caesar dressing
Dash coarsely ground pepper

1 In 10-inch skillet, heat oil over medium-high heat. Cook chicken in oil about 10 minutes, turning once, until brown on both sides. Remove chicken from skillet; keep warm.

2 Carefully add broth and water to hot skillet; heat to boiling. Stir in pasta; heat to boiling. Cook uncovered 8 to 10 minutes, stirring occasionally. Stir in broccoli, bell pepper and dressing (cut any large broccoli pieces in half).

3 Add chicken to pasta mixture; sprinkle with pepper. Heat to boiling; reduce heat. Simmer uncovered about 5 minutes or until vegetables are crisp-tender and juice of chicken is clear when center of thickest part is cut.

Chicken breasts are perfect when you're just cooking for two (or one), like in this quick-cooking chicken and pasta meal that makes just enough for two.

1 Serving: Calories 340 (Calories from Fat 60); Total Fat 7g (Saturated Fat 1.5g, Trans Fat 0g); Cholesterol 75mg; Sodium 410mg; Total Carbohydrate 34g (Dietary Fiber 5g, Sugars 4g); Protein 36g

Chicken Carbonara Deluxe

Prep Time: 30 min ■ Start to Finish: 30 min ■ 4 Servings

1 package (7 oz) spaghetti
8 slices bacon, cut into ½-inch pieces
1 medium onion, chopped (½ cup)
1 clove garlic, finely chopped
2 cups cut-up cooked chicken (about 1 lb)
½ cup grated Parmesan cheese
½ cup whipping cream

1 Cook and drain spaghetti as directed on package.

2 While spaghetti is cooking, cook bacon in 3-quart saucepan over low heat 8 to 10 minutes, stirring frequently, until crisp. Remove bacon from saucepan with slotted spoon; drain. Drain fat from saucepan, reserving 1 tablespoon in saucepan.

3 Cook onion and garlic in bacon fat over medium heat about 3 minutes, stirring frequently, until onion is tender. Stir in spaghetti, chicken, cheese and whipping cream. Cook, stirring occasionally, until heated through. Toss with bacon.

1 Serving: Calories 525 (Calories from Fat 215); Total Fat 24g (Saturated Fat 11g); Cholesterol 110mg; Sodium 460mg; Total Carbohydrate 44g (Dietary Fiber 2g); Protein 35g

Roasted Vegetable and Chicken Manicotti

Prep Time: 35 min ▪ Start to Finish: 1 hr 35 min ▪ 6 Servings

1 lb asparagus, cut into
    2-inch pieces (3 cups)
1 medium red bell pepper, cut into
    12 pieces
1 medium onion, cut into thin wedges
1 cup halved mushrooms
1 tablespoon olive or vegetable oil
1/2 teaspoon lemon-pepper seasoning

1/4 teaspoon salt
12 uncooked manicotti shells
1 envelope (1.8 oz) white sauce mix
2 1/4 cups milk
1/4 teaspoon dried marjoram leaves
1 1/2 cups shredded Havarti cheese
    (6 oz)
2 cups diced cooked chicken

1 Heat oven to 450°F. Toss the vegetables with oil, lemon-pepper seasoning and salt. Spread in ungreased jelly roll or roasting pan and roast 20 minutes or until vegetables are crisp-tender. Cool slightly. Coarsely chop vegetables.

2 Meanwhile, cook and drain manicotti as directed on package. In 1 1/2-quart saucepan, mix sauce mix and milk. Heat to boiling, stirring constantly. Stir in marjoram; remove from heat.

3 Reserve 1 cup vegetables for topping. Mix remaining vegetables, 1 cup of the cheese, the chicken and 1/2 cup of the sauce; spoon into manicotti shells. In bottom of ungreased rectangular baking dish, 13×9×2 inches, spread about 1/4 cup sauce. Arrange manicotti in dish; spoon over remaining sauce. Sprinkle with remaining 1 cup vegetables and 1/2 cup cheese.

4 Cover and bake 30 minutes. Uncover and bake about 10 minutes or until bubbly.

1 Serving: Calories 485 (Calories from Fat 225); Total Fat 25g (Saturated Fat 10g); Cholesterol 75mg; Sodium 670mg; Total Carbohydrate 39g (Dietary Fiber 3g); Protein 29g

Mexican Chicken–Sour Cream Lasagna

Prep Time: 30 min ■ Start to Finish: 1 hr 45 min ■ 8 Servings

12 uncooked lasagna noodles
2 cans (10³/₄ oz each) condensed
    cream of chicken soup
1 container (8 oz) sour cream
¹/₄ cup milk
1¹/₄ teaspoons ground cumin
¹/₂ teaspoon garlic powder
3 cups cubed cooked chicken
    (about 1¹/₂ lbs)
1 can (4.5 oz) chopped green chiles,
    undrained

8 to 10 medium green onions, sliced
    (about ¹/₂ cup)
¹/₂ cup chopped fresh cilantro or parsley
3 cups finely shredded Mexican-style
    Cheddar–Monterey Jack cheese
    blend (12 oz)
1 large red bell pepper, chopped (1 cup)
1 can (2.25 oz) sliced ripe olives, drained
1 cup crushed nacho cheese-flavor
    tortilla chips
Additional chopped or whole fresh
    cilantro leaves, if desired

1 Heat oven to 350°F. Spray bottom and sides of 13×9-inch (3-quart) glass baking dish with cooking spray. Cook and drain noodles as directed on package. Meanwhile, in large bowl, mix soup, sour cream, milk, cumin, garlic powder, chicken and chiles.

2 Spread about 1¹/₄ cups of the chicken mixture in baking dish. Top with 4 noodles. Spread 1¹/₄ cups chicken mixture over noodles; sprinkle with onions and cilantro. Sprinkle with 1 cup of the cheese.

3 Top with 4 noodles. Spread 1¹/₄ cups chicken mixture over noodles; sprinkle with bell pepper and olives. Sprinkle with 1 cup of the cheese. Top with 4 noodles; spread with remaining chicken mixture.

4 Bake uncovered 30 minutes; sprinkle with tortilla chips and remaining 1 cup cheese. Bake 15 to 30 minutes longer or until bubbly and hot in center. Sprinkle with additional cilantro. Let stand 15 minutes before cutting.

1 Serving: Calories 570 (Calories from Fat 280); Total Fat 32g (Saturated Fat 15g); Cholesterol 110mg; Sodium 1150mg; Total Carbohydrate 41g (Dietary Fiber 3g); Protein 33g

Spoon your favorite salsa over the lasagna for a touch of color.

Asian Chicken and Noodles

Prep Time: 25 min ■ Start to Finish: 25 min ■ 4 Servings

8 oz uncooked soba (buckwheat) noodles
¹/₂ lb boneless skinless chicken breasts, cut into thin slices
1 bag (16 oz) fresh stir-fry vegetables (broccoli, cauliflower, celery, carrots, snow
    pea pods and bell peppers) (4 cups)
¹/₄ cup fat-free chicken broth with 33% less sodium or water
¹/₂ cup teriyaki baste and glaze (from 12-oz bottle)
1 teaspoon dark sesame oil
¹/₄ teaspoon crushed red pepper flakes

1 Cook and drain noodles as directed on package.

2 While noodles are cooking, spray 10-inch skillet with cooking spray; heat over medium-high heat. Add chicken; cook 3 to 5 minutes, stirring frequently, or until no longer pink in center. Remove chicken from skillet. Add vegetables and broth to skillet. Heat to boiling. Cover; boil about 2 minutes or until vegetables are crisp-tender.

3 In small bowl, mix teriyaki glaze, oil and pepper flakes; add to vegetables in skillet. Stir in chicken. Heat to boiling. Serve chicken mixture over noodles.

Fresh stir-fry veggies from the produce aisle and purchased teriyaki baste and glaze make short work of this super-flavorful meal.

1 Serving: Calories 360 (Calories from Fat 40); Total Fat 4g (Saturated Fat 0.5g); Cholesterol 35mg; Sodium 980mg; Total Carbohydrate 57g (Dietary Fiber 5g); Protein 25g

Citrus-Ginger Chicken

Prep Time: 30 min ■ Start to Finish: 30 min ■ 4 Servings

> $^1/_2$ cup orange juice
> $^1/_4$ cup lime juice
> 2 tablespoons honey
> 1 teaspoon finely chopped gingerroot
> 1 teaspoon chopped fresh or $^1/_4$ teaspoon dried thyme leaves
> $^1/_4$ teaspoon salt
> $^1/_4$ teaspoon black and red pepper blend
> 4 boneless, skinless chicken breast halves (about 1$^1/_4$ lb)
> 1 tablespoon butter or margarine
> 1 medium seedless orange, peeled and cut into slices
> Additional fresh thyme leaves, if desired

1 Mix orange juice, lime juice, honey, gingerroot and 1 teaspoon thyme in medium bowl.

2 Spray 10-inch nonstick skillet with cooking spray; heat over medium-high heat. Sprinkle salt and pepper blend over chicken. Cook chicken in skillet 3 to 4 minutes, turning once, until brown. Stir in orange juice mixture. Heat to boiling; reduce heat to medium-low. Cover and cook 8 to 10 minutes or until chicken is no longer pink when centers of thickest pieces are cut. Remove chicken from skillet.

3 Heat sauce in skillet to boiling. Add butter. Cook, stirring constantly, until butter is melted and sauce is slightly thickened. Serve sauce over chicken and orange slices. Sprinkle with additional thyme.

Serve this chicken dish with rice or couscous to soak up the citrus-flavored sauce.

1 Serving: Calories 235 (Calories from Fat 65); Total Fat 7g (Saturated Fat 3g); Cholesterol 80mg; Sodium 240mg; Total Carbohydrate 17g (Dietary Fiber 1g); Protein 27g

Grilled Chicken with Chipotle-Peach Glaze

Prep Time: 10 min ▪ Start to Finish: 30 min ▪ 8 Servings

1/2 cup peach preserves
1/4 cup lime juice
1 chipotle chile in adobo sauce (from 7-oz can), seeded and chopped
1 teaspoon adobo sauce (from can of chiles)
2 tablespoons chopped fresh cilantro

1 teaspoon garlic-pepper blend
1/2 teaspoon ground cumin
1/2 teaspoon salt
8 boneless skinless chicken breasts (about 2 1/2 lb)
4 ripe peaches, cut in half and pitted
Cilantro sprigs, if desired

1 Heat coals or gas grill for medium heat.

2 In 1-quart saucepan, mix preserves, lime juice, chile and adobo sauce. Heat over low heat, stirring occasionally, until preserves are melted. Stir in chopped cilantro; set aside.

3 Mix garlic-pepper, cumin and salt together. Sprinkle both sides of chicken with mixture.

4 Grill chicken covered 15 to 20 minutes, turning once or twice and brushing with preserves mixture during last 2 minutes of grilling, until juice of chicken is clear when center of thickest part is cut. Add peach halves to grill for last 2 to 3 minutes of grilling just until heated.

5 In 1-quart saucepan, heat any remaining preserves mixture to boiling; boil and stir 1 minute. Serve with chicken and peaches. Garnish with cilantro sprigs.

1 Serving: Calories 250 (Calories from Fat 45); Total Fat 5g (Saturated Fat 1.5g); Cholesterol 85mg; Sodium 270mg; Total Carbohydrate 20g (Dietary Fiber 2g); Protein 32g

**When working with
canned chipotle** in adobo,
use caution and rubber gloves.

Cornmeal Chicken with Fresh Peach Salsa

Prep Time: 10 min ■ Start to Finish: 30 min ■ 4 Servings

Salsa
3 cups chopped peeled peaches
1 large tomato, chopped (1 cup)
1/4 cup chopped fresh cilantro
3 tablespoons vegetable oil
2 tablespoons white vinegar
1/4 teaspoon salt

Chicken
1/2 cup yellow cornmeal
1/2 teaspoon salt
1/4 teaspoon pepper
4 boneless skinless chicken breast halves (about 1 1/4 lb)
2 tablespoons vegetable oil

1 To make salsa, mix all of the ingredients.

2 To make chicken, mix cornmeal, salt and pepper. Coat chicken with cornmeal mixture.

3 Heat oil in 10-inch skillet over medium-high heat. Cook chicken in oil 15 to 20 minutes, turning once, until juice is no longer pink when centers of thickest pieces are cut. Serve with salsa.

1 serving: Calories 400 (Calories from Fat 180); Total Fat 20g (Saturated Fat 3g); Cholesterol 75mg; Sodium 510mg; Total Carbohydrate 31g (Dietary Fiber 5g); Protein 29g

Chicken Breasts Florentine

Prep Time: 20 min ■ Start to Finish: 1 hr 5 min ■ 4 Servings

2 cups uncooked egg noodles (4 oz)
3 tablespoons butter or margarine
3 tablespoons all-purpose flour
1/4 teaspoon pepper
1 cup milk
1 cup chicken broth
1 package (10 oz) frozen chopped spinach, thawed and squeezed to drain
1/2 cup grated Parmesan cheese
1/4 teaspoon ground nutmeg
4 boneless, skinless chicken breast halves (1 1/4 lb)
Additional ground nutmeg

1 Heat oven to 375°F. Spray rectangular pan, 11×7×1 1/2 inches, with cooking spray. Cook and drain noodles as directed on package.

2 Melt butter in 2-quart saucepan over medium heat. Stir in flour and pepper. Cook over medium heat, stirring constantly, until smooth and bubbly; remove from heat. Stir in milk and broth. Heat to boiling, stirring constantly. Boil and stir 1 minute; remove from heat.

3 Mix spinach, noodles, half of the sauce, 1/4 cup of the cheese and 1/4 teaspoon nutmeg. Spoon mixture into pan. Place chicken on spinach mixture. Pour remaining sauce over chicken. Sprinkle with remaining 1/4 cup cheese and additional nutmeg.

4 Cover and bake 30 minutes. Uncover and bake about 15 minutes longer or until light brown on top and juice of chicken is no longer pink when centers of thickest pieces are cut.

1 Serving: Calories 370 (Calories from Fat 120); Total Fat 13g (Saturated Fat 5g); Cholesterol 40mg; Sodium 850mg; Total Carbohydrate 39g (Dietary Fiber 2g); Protein 25g

Tarragon Chicken and Leeks

Prep Time: 25 min ▪ Start to Finish: 25 min ▪ 4 Servings

4 boneless, skinless chicken breast halves (about 1 lb)
2 medium leeks, sliced (1 cup)
²/₃ cup evaporated skimmed milk
1 tablespoon Dijon mustard
1¹/₂ teaspoons chopped fresh or ¹/₂ teaspoon dried tarragon leaves
1 teaspoon cornstarch

1 Spray 10-inch skillet with nonstick cooking spray; heat over medium-high heat. Cook chicken in skillet 12 to 14 minutes, turning once, until juice is no longer pink when centers of thickest pieces are cut. Remove chicken from skillet; keep warm.

2 Cook leeks in skillet about 3 minutes, stirring frequently, until crisp-tender. Mix remaining ingredients; stir into leeks. Heat to boiling, stirring occasionally. Boil and stir about 1 minute or until slightly thickened. Add chicken; heat through.

1 Serving: Calories 190 (Calories from Fat 35); Total Fat 4g (Saturated Fat 1g); Cholesterol 70mg; Sodium 170mg; Total Carbohydrate 10g (Dietary Fiber 1g); Protein 30g

Chicken in Fresh Herbs

Prep Time: 30 min ■ Start to Finish: 30 min ■ 4 Servings

4 boneless skinless chicken breasts (about 1¹/₄ lb)
1 medium shallot, chopped
¹/₄ cup chopped fresh chervil leaves
¹/₄ cup chopped fresh tarragon leaves
¹/₂ cup dry white wine or chicken broth
1 tablespoon lemon juice
¹/₂ teaspoon salt
Cracked pepper, if desired

1 Heat 10-inch skillet over medium-high heat until hot.

2 Cook all ingredients except pepper in skillet 15 to 20 minutes, turning chicken once, until juice of chicken is clear when center of thickest part is cut. Sprinkle with pepper.

1 Serving: Calories 170 (Calories from Fat 40); Total Fat 4.5g (Saturated Fat 1.5g); Cholesterol 85mg; Sodium 380mg; Total Carbohydrate 0g (Dietary Fiber 0g); Protein 31g

Chicken-Rice Skillet

Prep Time: 15 min ▪ Start to Finish: 20 min ▪ 4 Servings

1 tablespoon vegetable oil
1 1/4 lb boneless skinless chicken breasts, cut into 1-inch pieces
2 cups water
1 tablespoon butter or margarine
1 bag (1 lb) frozen broccoli, red peppers, onions and mushrooms (or other
    combination), thawed and drained
2 cups uncooked instant rice
1 teaspoon salt
1/4 teaspoon pepper
1 cup shredded Cheddar cheese (4 oz)

1 In 12-inch skillet, heat oil over medium-high heat. Cook chicken in oil 3 to 4 minutes, stirring occasionally, until no longer pink in center.

2 Add water and butter; heat to boiling. Stir in vegetables, rice, salt and pepper. Sprinkle with cheese; remove from heat.

3 Cover and let stand about 5 minutes or until water is absorbed.

1 Serving: Calories 580 (Calories from Fat 190); Total Fat 21g (Saturated Fat 9g); Cholesterol 125mg; Sodium 870mg; Total Carbohydrate 54g (Dietary Fiber 3g); Protein 45g

Layered Chicken–Black Bean Enchiladas

Prep Time: 25 min ▪ Start to Finish: 1 hr 5 min ▪ 6 Servings

2 cups chopped cooked chicken

2 tablespoons chopped fresh cilantro

1 (15-oz) can black beans, drained, rinsed

1 (4.5-oz) chopped green chiles

1 (10-oz) can enchilada sauce

8 (6-inch) corn tortillas

6 oz (1½ cups) shredded Colby–Monterey Jack cheese blend

1 (8-oz) container sour cream

1 Heat oven to 375°F. Spray 12×8-inch (2-quart) glass baking dish with nonstick cooking spray. In medium bowl, combine chicken, cilantro, black beans and chiles; mix well.

2 Spoon 2 tablespoons of the enchilada sauce in bottom of sprayed baking dish. Place 4 tortillas over enchilada sauce, overlapping as necessary. Spoon half of chicken mixture over tortillas; sprinkle with ½ cup cheese. Spoon half of remaining enchilada sauce and half of the sour cream randomly over cheese. Repeat layers. Cover with foil.

3 Bake at 375°F for 30 to 35 minutes or until thoroughly heated. Uncover; sprinkle remaining ½ cup cheese over casserole. Bake, uncovered, an additional 5 minutes or until cheese is melted. Let stand 10 minutes before serving.

1 Serving: Calories 440 (Calories from Fat 210); Total Fat 23g (Saturated Fat 12g); Cholesterol 85mg; Sodium 640mg; Total Carbohydrate 30g (Dietary Fiber 6g); Protein 28g

Sweet and Spicy Chicken Fajitas

Prep Time: 20 min ▪ Start to Finish: 20 min ▪ 4 Servings

1 tablespoon vegetable oil
1 lb boneless skinless chicken breast halves, cut into thin strips
½ cup salsa
¼ cup ketchup
1 to 2 tablespoons packed brown sugar
2 teaspoons Dijon mustard
4 jalapeno-flavored flour tortillas (8 inch), warmed

1 Heat oil in 12-inch skillet or wok over high heat. Add chicken; stir-fry 2 to 3 minutes or until brown.

2 Add salsa, ketchup, brown sugar and mustard; cook 3 to 4 minutes, stirring constantly, until chicken is no longer pink in center. Serve in tortillas.

Pop the package of chicken in the freezer for about
1½ hours before cutting. The chicken will be easier to cut if it's
partially frozen. To accompany these zesty fajitas, set out bowls
of shredded lettuce and chopped tomato, avocado and onion.

1 Serving: Calories 330 (Calories from Fat 90); Total Fat 10g (Saturated Fat 2g); Cholesterol 60mg; Sodium 560mg; Total Carbohydrate 33g (Dietary Fiber 2g); Protein 29g

Zesty Roasted Chicken and Potatoes

Prep Time: 10 min ■ Start to Finish: 35 min ■ 6 Servings

6 boneless skinless chicken breasts (about 1²/₃ lb)
1 lb small red potatoes, cut into fourths
¹/₃ cup mayonnaise or salad dressing
3 tablespoons Dijon mustard
¹/₂ teaspoon pepper
2 cloves garlic, finely chopped
Chopped fresh chives, if desired

1 Heat oven to 350°F. Spray 15×10×1-inch pan with cooking spray.

2 Place chicken and potatoes in pan. In small bowl, mix remaining ingredients except chives; brush over chicken and potatoes.

3 Bake uncovered 30 to 35 minutes or until potatoes are tender and juice of chicken is clear when center of thickest part is cut. Sprinkle with chives.

Want to make this lighter? Use low-fat mayonnaise for 9 grams of fat and 270 calories per serving.

1 Serving: Calories 380 (Calories from Fat 210); Total Fat 23g (Saturated Fat 5g); Cholesterol 95mg; Sodium 340mg; Total Carbohydrate 14g (Dietary Fiber 2g); Protein 28g

Spicy Southwest Chicken Kabobs

Prep Time: 10 min ▪ Start to Finish: 20 min ▪ 6 Servings

1 tablespoon garlic pepper
2 tablespoons olive or vegetable oil
4 small ears corn, husks removed
1 1/2 lb boneless skinless chicken breasts, cut into 1-inch cubes
2 medium yellow or red bell peppers, cut into 1 1/2-inch pieces
2/3 cup ranch dressing
1 canned chipotle chile in adobo sauce, chopped

1 Heat coals or gas grill for direct heat. Mix garlic pepper and oil. Cut each ear of corn into 3 pieces. Thread chicken, corn and bell peppers alternately on each of six 10- to 12-inch metal skewers, leaving 1/4-inch space between each piece. Brush kabobs with oil mixture.

2 Cover and grill kabobs 4 to 5 inches from medium heat 15 to 20 minutes, turning 2 or 3 times, until chicken is no longer pink in center.

3 Mix dressing and chile. Serve with kabobs.

Get a jump on dinner—cut the chicken and vegetables the night before, and refrigerate in plastic food-storage bags.

1 Serving: Calories 390 (Calories from Fat 205); Total Fat 23g (Saturated Fat 3g); Cholesterol 80mg; Sodium 400mg; Total Carbohydrate 20g (Dietary Fiber 2g); Protein 28g

Chicken with Apricots, Brown Rice and Barley

Prep Time: 20 min ▪ Start to Finish: 50 min ▪ 8 Servings

2 tablespoons vegetable oil
8 boneless skinless chicken breast halves (about 2 lb)
2 large carrots, shredded (2 cups)
2 cups sliced mushrooms (6 oz)
1 1/3 cups uncooked quick-cooking pearled barley
1 1/3 cups uncooked quick-cooking brown rice
2/3 cup chopped dried apricots
1/2 cup sliced green onions (5 medium)
2 2/3 cups chicken broth
2 tablespoons chopped fresh or 2 teaspoons dried thyme leaves
1/2 teaspoon salt
1/4 teaspoon ground red pepper (cayenne)
2 cans (5 1/2 oz each) apricot nectar

1 Heat oven to 350°F. Heat oil in Dutch oven over medium heat. Cook chicken in oil about 5 minutes or until brown on both sides. Stir in remaining ingredients. Heat to boiling; remove from heat.

2 Spoon mixture into ungreased rectangular baking dish, 13×9×2 inches. Cover and bake about 30 minutes or until barley and rice are tender and juice of chicken is no longer pink when centers of thickest pieces are cut.

1 Serving: Calories 455 (Calories from Fat 80); Total Fat 9g (Saturated Fat 2g); Cholesterol 65mg; Sodium 470mg; Total Carbohydrate 67g (Dietary Fiber 8g); Protein 35g

Chicken and Rice with Autumn Vegetables

Prep Time: 15 min ▪ Start to Finish: 30 min ▪ 4 Servings

1 package (about 6 oz) chicken-flavored rice mix or rice and vermicelli mix
2 cups 1-inch pieces butternut squash
1 medium zucchini, cut lengthwise in half, then crosswise into $^2/_3$-inch slices
1 medium red bell pepper, cut into 1-inch pieces (1 cup)
4 boneless, skinless chicken breast halves (about 1$^1/_4$ lb)
2 cups water
$^1/_2$ cup garlic-and-herb spreadable cheese

1 Heat oven to 425°F. Mix rice, contents of seasoning packet, squash, zucchini and bell pepper in ungreased rectangular pan, 13×9×2 inches.

2 Spray 10-inch skillet with cooking spray; heat over medium-high heat. Cook chicken in skillet 5 minutes, turning once, until brown. Remove chicken from skillet.

3 Add water to skillet; heat to boiling. Pour boiling water over rice mixture; stir to mix. Stir in cheese. Place chicken on rice mixture.

4 Cover and bake about 30 minutes or until liquid is absorbed and juice of chicken is no longer pink when centers of thickest pieces are cut.

1 Serving: Calories 340 (Calories from Fat 125); Total Fat 14g (Saturated Fat 7g); Cholesterol 105mg; Sodium 320mg; Total Carbohydrate 23g (Dietary Fiber 2g); Protein 32g

African Peanut–Chicken Soup

North African Chicken

Caribbean Chicken and Black Bean Salad

Chicken Satay with Peanut Sauce

Indonesian Chicken Breasts

Chicken Lo Mein

Teriyaki Chicken Stir-Fry

Indian Spiced Chicken and Chutney

Slow-Cooker Spanish Chicken

Chicken with Mole Sauce

Easy Mexican Chicken and Beans

Moroccan Spiced Chicken

Chicken Penne à la Marengo

Italian Chicken Risotto

Mediterranean Chicken Vegetable Kabobs

Chicken, Milan Style

Italian Mixed Grill

4

go global

African Peanut–Chicken Soup

Prep Time: 40 min ▪ Start to Finish: 40 min ▪ 6 Servings

1 tablespoon vegetable oil
1¼ lb boneless skinless chicken breasts, cut into 1-inch pieces
1 small onion, cut into thin wedges
1 clove garlic, finely chopped
2 medium dark orange sweet potatoes, peeled and coarsely chopped
1 medium green bell pepper, chopped (1 cup)
2 cans (14 oz each) chicken broth
1 can (11½ oz) tomato juice
½ teaspoon ground ginger
⅛ to ¼ teaspoon ground red pepper (cayenne)
½ cup crunchy peanut butter

1 Heat oil in 4-quart saucepan or Dutch oven over medium-high heat. Cook and stir chicken, onion and garlic in oil 4 to 5 minutes or until chicken is no longer pink in center.

2 Stir in remaining ingredients except peanut butter. Heat to boiling; reduce heat to low. Cover and simmer 10 to 12 minutes, stirring occasionally, until vegetables are tender.

3 Stir in peanut butter. Cook over low heat, stirring constantly, until peanut butter is blended and soup is hot.

Spice it up—plop a mound of hot cooked rice in the middle of each bowl of soup and sprinkle chopped peanuts, flaked coconut and sliced green onions over the top.

1 Serving: Calories 355 (Calories from Fat 155); Total Fat 17g (Saturated Fat 4g); Cholesterol 50mg; Sodium 980mg; Total Carbohydrate 22g (Dietary Fiber 4g); Protein 28g

North African Chicken

Prep Time: 25 min ▪ Start to Finish: 1 hr 25 min ▪ 4 Servings

North African Seasoning Mix

1/2 cup chopped fresh cilantro

1/4 cup chopped fresh mint leaves

1 tablespoon paprika

3/4 teaspoon salt

1/2 teaspoon saffron threads, crushed, or ground turmeric

Chicken

1/4 cup lemon juice

1/4 cup olive or vegetable oil

2 cloves garlic, finely chopped

4 boneless skinless chicken breast halves (about 1 lb)

1 To prepare the seasoning mix, combine all of the ingredients in storage container with tight-fitting lid. Refrigerate up to 5 days. Stir to mix before each use.

2 To prepare the chicken, mix 2 tablespoons of the mix, the lemon juice, oil and garlic in shallow glass dish. Add chicken; turn to coat with marinade. Cover and refrigerate at least 1 hour but no longer than 24 hours. Meanwhile, heat a charcoal or gas grill.

3 Remove chicken from marinade; reserve marinade. Cover and grill chicken 4 to 6 inches from medium coals 15 to 20 minutes, brushing with marinade and turning once, until juice of chicken is no longer pink when centers of thickest pieces are cut. Discard any remaining marinade.

1 Serving: Calories 215 (Calories from Fat 115); Total Fat 13g (Saturated Fat 2 g); Cholesterol 60mg; Sodium 160mg; Total Carbohydrate 1g (Dietary Fiber 0g); Protein 24g

Caribbean Chicken and Black Bean Salad

Prep Time: 20 min ▪ Start to Finish: 20 min ▪ 4 Servings

Spicy Lime Dressing

$1/4$ cup lime juice

2 tablespoons olive or vegetable oil

1 tablespoon honey

$1/2$ teaspoon chili powder

$1/4$ teaspoon ground cumin

$1/4$ teaspoon salt

2 to 3 drops red pepper sauce

Salad

2 cups cut-up cooked chicken (about 1 lb)

$1/4$ cup chopped fresh cilantro

1 large tomato, chopped (1 cup)

1 medium avocado, peeled and chopped

1 small yellow summer squash, chopped

1 can (15 oz) black beans, drained, rinsed

Leaf lettuce

1 In tightly covered container, shake all dressing ingredients until well blended.

2 In large bowl, toss all salad ingredients except lettuce. Pour dressing over salad; toss. Serve on lettuce leaves.

On the run? Pick up a roasted chicken from the deli for the salad. One roasted chicken will yield about 2 to $2^{1/2}$ cups of cut-up chicken.

1 Serving: Calories 370 (Calories from Fat 170); Total Fat 19g (Saturated Fat 4g); Cholesterol 60mg; Sodium 500mg; Total Carbohydrate 31g (Dietary Fiber 8g); Protein 27g

Chicken Satay with Peanut Sauce

Prep Time: 35 min ■ Start to Finish: 2 hrs 25 min ■ 4 Servings

Chicken Satay

3 tablespoons lime juice

1 teaspoon curry powder

2 teaspoons honey

1/2 teaspoon ground coriander

1/2 teaspoon ground cumin

1/8 teaspoon salt

2 cloves garlic, finely chopped

1 lb boneless skinless chicken
    breast halves, cut into 1-inch cubes

1 medium red bell pepper, cut into
    1¼ inch pieces

4 medium green onions, cut into
    2-inch pieces

Peanut Sauce

1/2 cup creamy peanut butter

1/2 cup water

2 tablespoons lime juice

1/2 teaspoon ground coriander

1/2 teaspoon ground cumin

1/8 teaspoon salt

1/8 teaspoon ground red pepper
    (cayenne), if desired

2 cloves garlic, finely chopped

1 In lidded glass or plastic dish, stir lime juice, curry powder, honey, coriander, cumin, salt and garlic until well mixed. Add chicken and stir to coat. Cover and refrigerate 2 hours, stirring occasionally.

2 Meanwhile, make sauce: In 1-quart saucepan, mix all sauce ingredients with wire whisk. Heat over medium heat, stirring occasionally, until smooth and warm.

3 To cook the chicken, set oven to broil. Spray rack in broiler pan with cooking spray. Remove chicken from marinade; reserve marinade. Thread chicken, 1 bell pepper piece and 2 onion pieces on each of eight 8-inch skewers,* leaving space between each piece. Place skewers on rack in broiler pan.

4 Broil with tops about 3 inches from heat 4 minutes. Turn; brush with marinade. Broil 4 to 5 minutes longer or until chicken is no longer pink in center. Discard any remaining marinade. Serve with sauce.

* If using bamboo skewers, soak in water at least 30 minutes before using to prevent burning.

1 Serving: Calories 330 (Calories from Fat 140); Total Fat 15g (Saturated Fat 5g); Cholesterol 70mg; Sodium 500mg; Total Carbohydrate 17g (Dietary Fiber 2g); Protein 32g

Indonesian Chicken Breasts

Prep Time: 35 min ▪ Start to Finish: 1 hr 35 min ▪ 4 Servings

1/2 cup orange juice
1/4 cup peanut butter
2 teaspoons curry powder
4 boneless skinless chicken breast halves (about 1 lb)
1 medium red bell pepper, cut in half
1/4 cup shredded coconut
1/4 cup currants
Hot cooked rice, if desired

1 Beat orange juice, peanut butter and curry powder in medium nonmetal bowl, using wire whisk. Add chicken, turning to coat with marinade. Cover and refrigerate, turning once, at least 1 hour but no longer than 24 hours.

2 Heat coals or gas grill. Remove chicken from marinade; discard marinade. Cover and grill chicken and bell pepper 4 to 6 inches from medium heat 15 to 20 minutes, turning once, until chicken is no longer pink in center. To serve, cut chicken breasts diagonally into 1/2-inch slices and bell pepper into 1/2-inch strips. Top chicken and bell pepper with coconut and currants. Serve with rice.

1 Serving: Calories 315 (Calories from Fat 125); Total Fat 14g (Saturated Fat 5g); Cholesterol 70mg; Sodium 160mg; Total Carbohydrate 19g (Dietary Fiber 2g); Protein 30g

Chicken Lo Mein

Prep Time: 16 min ▪ Start to Finish: 16 min ▪ 4 Servings

1 package (8 oz) lo mein noodles
1 pound boneless skinless chicken breast halves, cut into thin strips
1/2 cup stir-fry sauce
1/4 cup chicken broth
1/4 teaspoon crushed red pepper
1 bag (16 oz) frozen baby pea blend

1 Cook and drain noodles as directed on package.

2 While noodles are cooking, spray 10-inch skillet with cooking spray; heat over medium-high heat. Add chicken; stir-fry 2 to 3 minutes or until brown.

3 Stir in stir-fry sauce, broth and red pepper. Heat to boiling. Stir in frozen vegetables. Heat to boiling; reduce heat. Simmer uncovered about 5 minutes or until chicken is no longer pink in center and vegetables are tender.

4 Serve chicken mixture over noodles.

In a pinch, you can use angel hair pasta instead of lo mein noodles.

1 Serving: Calories 310 (Calories from Fat 35); Total Fat 4g (Saturated Fat 1g); Cholesterol 70mg; Sodium 1540mg; Total Carbohydrate 42g (Dietary Fiber 4g); Protein 31g

Teriyaki Chicken Stir-Fry

Prep Time: 15 min ▪ Start to Finish: 15 min ▪ 4 Servings

1 lb boneless skinless chicken breast strips for stir-fry
½ cup teriyaki baste and glaze
3 tablespoons lemon juice
1 bag (1 lb) frozen broccoli, carrots, water chestnuts and red peppers
    (or other combination)
Hot cooked rice, couscous, or noodles, if desired

1 Spray 12-inch nonstick skillet with cooking spray; heat over medium-high heat. Cook chicken 3 to 4 minutes, stirring frequently, until chicken is no longer pink in center.

2 Stir remaining ingredients except rice into chicken. Heat to boiling, stirring constantly; reduce heat to low. Cover and simmer about 6 minutes or until vegetables are crisp-tender. Serve with rice.

It's easy to confuse teriyaki baste and glaze with teriyaki sauce or marinade. The first is a thick and brown-colored sauce, while the second has a watery consistency. You'll want the baste and glaze for this recipe.

1 Serving: Calories 245 (Calories from Fat 65); Total Fat 7g (Saturated Fat 2g); Cholesterol 60mg; Sodium 1480mg; Total Carbohydrate 21g (Dietary Fiber 3g); Protein 28g

Indian Spiced Chicken and Chutney

Prep Time: 5 min ■ Start to Finish: 1 hr 25 min ■ 4 Servings

Spicy Yogurt Marinade
$1/2$ cup plain yogurt

1 tablespoon lemon juice

2 teaspoons grated gingerroot

$1/2$ teaspoon paprika

$1/2$ teaspoon ground coriander

$1/2$ teaspoon salt

$1/4$ teaspoon ground red pepper (cayenne)

$1/8$ teaspoon ground cloves

Chicken and Chutney
4 boneless skinless chicken breasts (about $1^1/4$ lb)

$1/2$ cup mango chutney

Hot cooked basmati rice or regular long-grain rice, if desired

1 In small bowl, mix all marinade ingredients.

2 Place chicken in resealable plastic food-storage bag or shallow glass or plastic dish. Pour marinade over chicken; turn chicken to coat with marinade. Seal bag or cover dish and refrigerate 1 hour.

3 In 12-inch skillet, cook chicken and marinade over medium-high heat 15 to 20 minutes, turning chicken once, until juice of chicken is clear when center of thickest part is cut. Top with chutney. Serve with rice.

Have leftover mango chutney? It makes a great spread for sandwiches, or serve it with cold roast pork, chicken, or turkey.

1 Serving: Calories 230 (Calories from Fat 45); Total Fat 5g (Saturated Fat 1.5g); Cholesterol 85mg; Sodium 410mg; Total Carbohydrate 13g (Dietary Fiber 0g); Protein 33g

Slow-Cooker Spanish Chicken

Prep Time: 15 min ▪ Start to Finish: 8 hrs 15 min ▪ 6 Servings

1³/₄ lb boneless skinless chicken breasts, cut into 1-inch pieces

1 lb turkey Italian sausages, cut into 1-inch pieces

1 large red bell pepper, chopped (1¹/₂ cups)

1 large onion, chopped (1 cup)

2 cloves garlic, finely chopped

1 teaspoon dried oregano leaves

¹/₂ to 1 teaspoon crushed red pepper

1 can (28 oz) diced tomatoes, undrained

1 can (6 oz) tomato paste

1 can (14 oz) artichoke heart quarters, drained

1 can (4 oz) sliced ripe olives, drained

3 cups hot cooked rice

1 In 3¹/₂ to 4 quart slow cooker, mix all ingredients except artichoke hearts, olives and rice.

2 Cover and cook on low heat setting 6 to 8 hours.

3 Stir in artichoke hearts and olives; heat through. Serve with rice.

1 Serving: Calories 490 (Calories from Fat 120); Total Fat 14g (Saturated Fat 3.5g); Cholesterol 120mg; Sodium 1860mg; Total Carbohydrate 46g (Dietary Fiber 8g); Protein 47g

Chicken with Mole Sauce

Prep Time: 35 min ■ Start to Finish: 2 hrs 35 min ■ 6 Servings

Chicken

4 cups water
1/3 cup salt
1/3 cup packed dark brown sugar
1 tablespoon cumin seed
1 tablespoon chili powder
1 lime, thinly sliced
1 cup strong-brewed coffee, at room temperature
6 boneless skinless chicken breasts (about 1 3/4 lb)
2 tablespoons vegetable oil

Mole Sauce

1 medium onion, thinly sliced
2 cloves garlic, finely chopped
1 can (28 oz) crushed tomatoes
1 1/4 cups chicken broth
1 tablespoon creamy peanut butter
1 teaspoon granulated sugar
1/2 teaspoon ground cumin
Dash of ground cinnamon
1 oz unsweetened baking chocolate
2 chipotle chiles in adobo sauce chopped
Salt and pepper, if desired

1 In 2-quart saucepan, heat water, salt, brown sugar, cumin seed, chili powder and lime slices over medium heat, stirring occasionally, until salt and brown sugar are dissolved. Remove from heat and stir in coffee. Cool mixture to room temperature.

2 Place chicken in large bowl and pour cooled coffee mixture over chicken. Cover and refrigerate 2 to 3 hours.

3 In 12-inch skillet, heat oil over medium heat. Remove chicken from marinade, pat dry on paper towels (discard marinade) and brown in skillet, 5 to 6 minutes, turning once, or until golden brown. Place chicken on plate.

4 In same skillet, cook onion 5 minutes, until soft and lightly browned. Add garlic and cook 30 seconds or until fragrant. Add tomatoes, broth, peanut butter, granulated sugar, ground cumin, cinnamon, chocolate and chiles and cook 3 minutes, stirring occasionally, until mixture simmers and peanut butter and chocolate are melted.

5 Reduce heat to medium-low and nestle chicken breasts in sauce. Cook uncovered 15 to 20 minutes, stirring occasionally, until sauce thickens and chicken is no longer pink in center. Add salt and pepper if necessary.

1 Serving: Calories 320 (Calories from Fat 120); Total Fat 14g (Saturated Fat 4g); Cholesterol 80mg; Sodium 2130mg; Total Carbohydrate 15g (Dietary Fiber 3g); Protein 33g

Easy Mexican Chicken and Beans

Prep Time: 20 min ▪ Start to Finish: 20 min ▪ 4 Servings

2 cups cooked chicken breast (about 1 lb), cut into strips
1 envelope (1¼ oz) taco seasoning mix
1 can (15 to 16 oz) black or pinto beans, rinsed and drained
1 can (11 oz) whole kernel corn with red and green peppers, undrained
¼ cup water

1 Mix together all ingredients in 2-quart saucepan.

2 Cook over medium-high heat 8 to 10 minutes, stirring frequently, until sauce is slightly thickened.

Turn this dish into a weeknight fiesta! Serve with flour tortillas, sour cream, salsa, black olives and green chiles and let everyone make their own wrap.

1 Serving: Calories 335 (Calories from Fat 70); Total Fat 8g (Saturated Fat 2g); Cholesterol 75mg; Sodium 950mg; Total Carbohydrate 44g (Dietary Fiber 8g); Protein 35g

Moroccan Spiced Chicken

Prep Time: 30 min ▪ Start to Finish: 30 min ▪ 4 Servings

1 tablespoon paprika

$^1/_2$ teaspoon salt

$^1/_2$ teaspoon ground cumin

$^1/_4$ teaspoon ground allspice

$^1/_4$ teaspoon ground cinnamon

4 boneless skinless chicken breasts (about 1 $^1/_4$ lb)

1 tablespoon vegetable oil

2 cups water

1 teaspoon vegetable oil

1$^1/_2$ cups uncooked couscous

$^1/_4$ cup raisins, if desired

1 small papaya, peeled, seeded and sliced

1 In small bowl, mix paprika, salt, cumin, allspice and cinnamon. Coat both sides of chicken with spice mixture.

2 In 10-inch skillet, heat 1 tablespoon oil over medium heat. Cook chicken in oil 15 to 20 minutes, turning once, until juice of chicken is clear when center of thickest part is cut.

3 Meanwhile, in 2-quart saucepan, heat water and 1 teaspoon oil just to boiling. Stir in couscous; remove from heat. Cover; let stand 5 minutes. Fluff couscous before serving; stir in raisins. Serve chicken with couscous and papaya.

1 Serving: Calories 470 (Calories from Fat 90); Total Fat 10g (Saturated Fat 2g.); Cholesterol 85mg; Sodium 380mg; Total Carbohydrate 55g (Dietary Fiber 5g); Protein 40g

Round out the meal with warmed pita folds drizzled with olive oil or melted butter or with Middle Eastern flatbread.

Chicken Penne à la Marengo

Prep Time: 40 min   Start to Finish: 40 min   4 Servings

1 lb boneless skinless chicken breasts cut into 1-inch pieces
1 can (14½ oz) chicken broth
2 cups uncooked penne pasta (6 oz)
1 medium green bell pepper, cut into 1-inch pieces (1 cup)
1 can (14½ oz) Italian-style stewed tomatoes, undrained
¼ cup dry white wine or chicken broth
1 tablespoon tomato paste
1 can (2¼ oz) sliced ripe olives, drained

1 Spray 12-inch nonstick skillet with cooking spray; heat over medium-high heat. Add chicken; stir-fry 2 to 3minutes or until brown.

2 Stir in broth; heat to boiling. Stir in pasta and bell pepper. Heat to boiling; reduce heat to medium. Cover and cook 10 minutes, stirring occasionally.

3 Stir in tomatoes, wine and tomato paste. Cook uncovered 5 to 10 minutes, stirring occasionally, until chicken is no longer pink in center and pasta is tender. Stir in olives.

If you like your sauce a little thicker, start with 1 tablespoon of tomato paste and then add an additional tablespoon.

1 Serving: Calories 405 (Calories from Fat 55); Total Fat 6g (Saturated Fat 1g); Cholesterol 50mg; Sodium 950mg; Total Carbohydrate 62g (Dietary Fiber 4g); Protein 30g

Italian Chicken Risotto

Prep Time: 37 min ▪ Start to Finish: 37 min ▪ 6 Servings

1 tablespoon olive or vegetable oil
2 medium zucchini, cut into julienne strips
2 medium bell peppers, cut into julienne strips
1 medium onion, thinly sliced
2 cups uncooked Arborio rice
3²/₃ cups chicken broth
1 cup half-and-half
¹/₄ teaspoon pepper
2 cups cut-up cooked chicken
2 tablespoons freshly grated Parmesan cheese

1 Heat oil in 12-inch skillet or 4-quart Dutch oven over medium-high heat. Cook zucchini, bell peppers and onion in oil 5 to 7 minutes, stirring frequently, until crisp-tender. Remove mixture from skillet.

2 Add rice to skillet. Cook uncovered, stirring frequently, until rice begins to brown; reduce heat to medium.

3 Mix broth, half-and-half and pepper; pour ¹/₂ cup broth mixture over rice. Cook uncovered, stirring occasionally, until liquid is absorbed.

4 Continue cooking 15 to 20 minutes, adding broth mixture ¹/₂ cup at a time and stirring occasionally, until rice is tender and creamy, and adding chicken and zucchini mixture with the last addition of broth. Sprinkle with cheese.

Company coming? Make this dish by substituting ¹/₃ cup dry white wine for ¹/₃ cup of the chicken broth.

1 Serving: Calories 445 (Calories from Fat 110); Total Fat 12g (Saturated Fat 5g); Cholesterol 55mg; Sodium 730mg; Total Carbohydrate 61g (Dietary Fiber 2g); Protein 25g

Mediterranean Chicken Vegetable Kabobs

Prep Time: 25 min ■ Start to Finish: 55 min ■ 4 Servings

Rosemary Lemon Marinade
1/4 cup lemon juice
3 tablespoons olive or vegetable oil
2 teaspoons chopped fresh or
    1 teaspoon dried rosemary leaves
1/2 teaspoon salt
1/4 teaspoon pepper
4 cloves garlic, finely chopped

Chicken Kabobs
1 lb boneless skinless chicken
    breasts, cut into 1 1/2-inch pieces
1 medium red bell pepper, cut into
    1-inch pieces
1 medium zucchini or yellow summer
    squash, cut into 1-inch pieces
1 medium red onion, cut into wedges
1 lb asparagus spears
1/4 cup feta cheese

1 Make the marinade by combining all of the ingredients in shallow glass or plastic dish. Add chicken; stir to coat with marinade. Cover dish and refrigerate, stirring chicken occasionally, at least 30 minutes but no longer than 6 hours.

2 Heat coals or gas grill for direct heat. Remove chicken from marinade; reserve marinade. Thread chicken, bell pepper, zucchini and onion alternately on each of four 15-inch metal skewers, leaving space between each piece. Brush vegetables with marinade.

3 Cover and grill kabobs 4 to 6 inches from medium heat 10 to 15 minutes, turning and brushing frequently with marinade, until chicken is no longer pink in center. Add asparagus to grill for last 5 minutes, turning occasionally, until crisp-tender. Discard any remaining marinade.

4 Sprinkle cheese over kabobs and serve with asparagus.

1 Serving: Calories 260 (Calories from Fat 115); Total Fat 13g (Saturated Fat 3g); Cholesterol 75mg; Sodium 370mg; Total Carbohydrate 10g (Dietary Fiber 3g); Protein 29g

For a great side dish toss cooked rosamarina (orzo) pasta with chopped fresh herbs. Thyme and Italian parsley are terrific.

Chicken, Milan Style

Prep Time: 35 min   Start to Finish: 35 min   6 Servings

6 boneless skinless chicken breast halves (about 1³/₄ lb)

¹/₂ teaspoon salt

¹/₄ teaspoon pepper

2 eggs, beaten

1 tablespoon fresh lemon juice

¹/₃ cup all-purpose flour

1 cup Italian-style dry bread crumbs

¹/₂ cup butter or margarine

1 lemon, cut into wedges

Chopped fresh parsley or parsley sprigs, if desired

1 Flatten each chicken breast half to ¹/₄-inch thickness between sheets of plastic wrap or waxed paper. Sprinkle with salt and pepper. Mix eggs and lemon juice. Coat chicken with flour; shake off excess flour. Dip chicken into egg mixture, then coat with bread crumbs; shake off excess crumbs.

2 Melt butter in 12-inch skillet over medium heat. Cook chicken in butter 10 to 15 minutes, turning once, until chicken is golden brown on outside and no longer pink in center.

3 Place chicken on warm platter; pour any remaining butter from skillet over chicken. Garnish with lemon wedges and parsley.

1 Serving: Calories 390 (Calories from Fat 200); Total Fat 22g (Saturated Fat 11g); Cholesterol 190mg; Sodium 530mg; Total Carbohydrate 16g (Dietary Fiber 1g); Protein 33g

Italian Mixed Grill

Prep Time: 50 min ■ Start to Finish: 1 hr 50 min ■ 8 Servings

Herbed Lemon Oil
1/2 cup olive or vegetable oil
3 tablespoons lemon juice
3 tablespoons chopped fresh parsley
1 tablespoon chopped fresh or
    1 teaspoon dried rosemary leaves
2 teaspoons chopped fresh or
    1/2 teaspoon dried thyme leaves
1/2 teaspoon salt

1/4 teaspoon pepper
2 large cloves garlic, finely chopped
Mixed Grill
4 fresh Italian sausages (about 1 lb)
1/2 cup water
1 small onion, chopped (1/4 cup)
4 boneless skinless chicken breasts
1-lb beef boneless top sirloin steak,
    about 1 inch thick

1 In small bowl, mix all Herbed Lemon Oil ingredients. Cover and let stand at least 1 hour to blend flavors.

2 In 2-quart microwavable casserole, place sausages, water and onion. Cover and microwave on High 5 minutes; rearrange sausages. Re-cover and microwave on Medium (50%) 5 to 7 minutes or until sausages are no longer pink in center. Remove sausages; discard onion and water

3 Brush grill rack with vegetable oil. Heat coals or gas grill for direct heat. Brush all sides of chicken, beef and sausages with oil mixture.

4 Grill meats uncovered over medium heat, brushing frequently with oil mixture and turning occasionally, for the following times: Grill beef 5 minutes. Add chicken; grill beef and chicken 5 minutes. Add sausages; grill beef, chicken and sausages 4 to 15 minutes or until each are done according to the following guidelines: Cook beef to desired doneness, about 17 to 21 minutes total grilling time. Chicken is done when juice is clear when center of thickest part is cut, about 15 to 20 minutes total grilling time. Sausages are done when no longer pink in center, about 12 to 14 minutes total grilling time. Discard any remaining oil mixture.

5 To serve, cut sausages and chicken pieces in half, and cut beef into slices.

1 Serving: Calories 350 (Calories from Fat 210); Total Fat 24g (Saturated Fat 6g); Cholesterol 95mg; Sodium 480mg; Total Carbohydrate 2g (Dietary Fiber 0g); Protein 32g

Buffalo-Style Chicken Nuggets

Apricot-Glazed Coconut-Chicken Bites

Chicken BLT Sandwiches

Easy Chicken Chili

Easy Chicken Alfredo

Skillet Chicken Parmigiana

Linguine Pasta with Spicy Chicken Sauce

Chicken in Brandy Cream Sauce

Tequila Chicken with Fettuccine

Lemon-Basil Chicken and Vegetables

Thai-Style Coconut Chicken

Pineapple-Glazed Spicy Chicken Breasts

Caramelized-Garlic Chicken

Dijon Chicken Smothered in Mushrooms

Chicken Marsala

5

restaurant favorites at home

Buffalo-Style Chicken Nuggets

Prep Time: 10 min ■ Start to Finish: 25 min ■ 4 Servings

1½ cups Corn Chex® cereal
½ cup Original Bisquick mix
2 teaspoons paprika
¼ teaspoon seasoned salt
¼ teaspoon ground red pepper (cayenne)
1 tablespoon vegetable oil
1 teaspoon red pepper sauce
1 lb boneless skinless chicken breasts, cut into 2-inch pieces
¼ cup ranch dressing

1 Heat oven to 425°F. In 1-gallon resealable food-storage plastic bag, crush cereal with rolling pin. Add Bisquick mix, paprika, seasoned salt and red pepper to cereal; mix well.

2 In small bowl, mix oil and red pepper sauce. Coat chicken pieces with oil mixture.

3 Shake about 6 chicken pieces at a time in bag of cereal mixture until coated. Shake off any extra mixture. On ungreased cookie sheet, place chicken pieces in single layer.

4 Bake about 10 minutes or until chicken is no longer pink in center. Serve chicken with dressing.

1 Serving: Calories 340 (Calories from Fat 150); Total Fat 17g (Saturated Fat 3g); Cholesterol 75mg; Sodium 590mg; Total Carbohydrate 20g (Dietary Fiber 1g); Protein 27g

Apricot-Glazed Coconut-Chicken Bites

Prep Time: 15 min ▪ Start to Finish: 45 min ▪ About 3 Dozen Appetizers

Coconut-Chicken Bites

1/2 cup sweetened condensed milk
2 tablespoons Dijon mustard
1 1/2 cups Original Bisquick
2/3 cup flaked coconut
1/2 teaspoon salt
1/2 teaspoon paprika
1 lb boneless skinless chicken breast halves, cut into 1-inch pieces
1/4 cup margarine or butter, melted
Hot mustard, if desired

Apricot Glaze

1/2 cup apricot spreadable fruit
2 tablespoons honey
2 tablespoons Dijon mustard
1 tablespoon white vinegar

1 Heat oven to 425°F. Mix milk and Dijon mustard. Mix Bisquick, coconut, salt and paprika. Dip chicken into milk mixture, then coat with Bisquick.

2 Pour 2 tablespoons of the melted margarine in jelly roll pan, 15 1/2 ×10 1/2 × 1 inch. Place coated chicken in pan. Drizzle remaining margarine over chicken. Bake uncovered 20 minutes.

3 To make glaze, stir all ingredients until blended. Turn chicken; brush with glaze. Bake 10 to 15 minutes longer or until chicken is no longer pink in center and glaze is bubbly. Serve with hot mustard.

1 Appetizer: Calories 80 (Calories from Fat 25); Total Fat 3g (Saturated Fat 1g); Cholesterol 5mg; Sodium 160mg; Total Carbohydrate 10g (Dietary Fiber 0g); Protein 3g

Chicken BLT Sandwiches

Prep Time: 30 min ▪ Start to Finish: 30 min ▪ 4 Sandwiches

4 boneless skinless chicken breast halves (about 1¼ lb)
¼ cup Thousand Island dressing
4 whole wheat sandwich buns, split
4 lettuce leaves
8 slices tomato
4 slices bacon, cooked, drained and broken in half

1 Heat coals or gas grill for direct heat. Cover and grill chicken 4 to 6 inches from medium heat 15 to 20 minutes, turning once or twice, until juice of chicken is no longer pink when centers of thickest pieces are cut.

2 Spread dressing on cut sides of buns. Layer lettuce, chicken, tomato and bacon on bottoms of buns. Top with tops of buns.

Save some time—looked for already-cooked bacon. It's in the supermarket with the regular bacon. All you have to do is reheat it in the microwave oven.

1 Serving: Calories 320 (Calories from Fat 125); Total Fat 14g (Saturated Fat 3g); Cholesterol 80mg; Sodium 450mg; Total Carbohydrate 20g (Dietary Fiber 3g); Protein 32g

Easy Chicken Chili

Prep Time: 35 min ▪ Start to Finish: 35 min ▪ 6 Servings

1 lb boneless skinless chicken breasts, diced
2 cans (15 to 16 oz each) kidney beans, drained
1 can (28 oz) whole tomatoes, undrained
$^1/_3$ cup chopped onion
1 tablespoon chili powder

Mix all ingredients in 3-quart saucepan, breaking up tomatoes. Heat to boiling, stirring occasionally; reduce heat. Simmer uncovered about 20 minutes, stirring occasionally, until chicken is no longer pink in center and flavors are well blended.

1 Serving: Calories 195 (Calories from Fat 25); Total Fat 3g (Saturated Fat 1g); Cholesterol 40mg; Sodium 620mg; Total Carbohydrate 24g (Dietary Fiber 8g); Protein 24g

Easy Chicken Alfredo

Prep Time: 21 min ■ Start to Finish: 21 min ■ 4 Servings

2 tablespoons olive or vegetable oil
1¼ pounds boneless skinless chicken breasts, cut into thin strips
2 medium zucchini, sliced (4 cups)
1 large red bell pepper, cut into thin strips (1 cup)
1 container (10 oz) refrigerated Alfredo sauce
Grated fresh Parmesan cheese

Heat oil in 12-inch skillet over medium-high heat. Cook chicken in oil
5 to 6 minutes, stirring occasionally, until chicken is no longer pink in center.
Add zucchini and bell pepper; cook about 5 minutes, stirring frequently, until
vegetables are crisp-tender. Stir in Alfredo sauce.
Sprinkle with cheese.

Be saucy—you can make this meal lots of times with
different flavored sauces. Try experimenting with
some of the refrigerated ones available, such as
marinara, sun-dried tomato pesto or clam sauce.

1 Serving: Calories 575 (Calories from Fat 370); Total Fat 41g (Saturated Fat 21g); Cholesterol 165mg;
Sodium 570mg; Total Carbohydrate 15g (Dietary Fiber 3g); Protein 39g

Skillet Chicken Parmigiana

Prep Time: 25 min ▪ Start to Finish: 25 min ▪ 4 Servings

4 boneless skinless chicken breast halves (about 1 lb)
$1/3$ cup Italian-style dry bread crumbs
$1/3$ cup grated Parmesan cheese
1 egg, beaten
2 tablespoons olive or vegetable oil
2 cups spaghetti sauce
$1/2$ cup shredded mozzarella cheese (2 oz)

1 Flatten chicken to $1/4$-inch thickness between plastic wrap or waxed paper using meat mallet or rolling pin. Mix bread crumbs and Parmesan cheese. Dip chicken into egg; coat with bread crumb mixture.

2 Heat oil in 12-inch skillet over medium-high heat. Cook chicken in oil 10 to 15 minutes, turning once, until juice is no longer pink when centers of thickest pieces are cut. Add spaghetti sauce. Reduce heat to low. Cook 2 to 3 minutes or until sauce is hot. Sprinkle mozzarella cheese over chicken. Serve with hot cooked pasta if desired.

1 Serving: Calories 405 (Calories from Fat 190); Total Fat 21g (Saturated Fat 6g); Cholesterol 135mg; Sodium 1170mg; Total Carbohydrate 19g (Dietary Fiber 2g); Protein 37g

Linguine Pasta with Spicy Chicken Sauce

Prep Time: 30 min ■ Start to Finish: 30 min ■ 4 Servings

8 oz uncooked linguine
2 tablespoons olive or vegetable oil
2 cloves garlic, finely chopped
2 teaspoons anchovy paste
1 red jalapeño chile, seeded and finely chopped
2 tablespoons chopped sun-dried tomatoes packed in oil
1 tablespoon chopped fresh or 1 teaspoon dried oregano leaves
1/2 lb boneless skinless chicken breasts, cut into 1-inch pieces
2 medium red or yellow bell peppers, cut into 1×1/4-inch strips
1/3 cup dry red wine or chicken broth
1/2 cup freshly grated or shredded Parmesan cheese

1 Cook and drain linguine as directed on package.

2 Meanwhile, in 12-inch skillet, heat oil over medium-high heat. Cook garlic, anchovy paste, chile and tomatoes in oil about 5 minutes, stirring frequently, until garlic just begins to turn golden.

3 Stir in oregano, chicken, bell peppers and wine. Cover and cook about 10 minutes, stirring occasionally, until chicken is no longer pink in center.

4 Add linguine and 1/4 cup of the cheese to mixture in skillet; toss until linguine is evenly coated. Sprinkle with remaining 1/4 cup cheese.

1 Serving: Calories 420 (Calories from Fat 125); Total Fat 14g (Saturated Fat 4g); Cholesterol 35mg; Sodium 490mg; Total Carbohydrate 52g (Dietary Fiber 3g); Protein 24g

Chicken in Brandy Cream Sauce

Prep Time: 32 min ▪ Start to Finish: 32 min ▪ 4 Servings

1 tablespoon olive or vegetable oil
4 boneless skinless chicken breasts (about 1¼ lb)
1 package (8 oz) sliced fresh mushrooms (3 cups)
4 medium green onions, chopped (¼ cup)
¼ teaspoon salt
¼ cup brandy or chicken broth
½ cup whipping cream
Hot cooked spinach fettuccine or regular fettuccine

1 In 10-inch skillet, heat oil over medium-high heat. Cook chicken in oil 10 to 15 minutes, turning once, until chicken is clear when center of thickest part is cut.

2 Stir in mushrooms, onions, salt and brandy. Cook 4 to 5 minutes or until mushrooms are tender and most of the liquid has evaporated.

3 Gradually stir in whipping cream. Cook about 2 minutes or until hot. Serve over fettuccine.

Who knew you could make an elegant dish so fast? Betty did!

1 Serving: Calories 310 (Calories from Fat 160); Total Fat 17g (Saturated Fat 8g); Cholesterol 120mg; Sodium 240mg; Total Carbohydrate 4g (Dietary Fiber 1g); Protein 34g

Tequila Chicken with Fettuccine

Prep Time: 25 min ■ Start to Finish: 45 min ■ 6 Servings

¼ cup tequila or chicken broth
¼ cup frozen (thawed) limeade
1 tablespoon grated lime peel
1½ lb boneless skinless chicken breast halves, cut into 1½× ½-inch strips
1 small yellow bell pepper, cut into ¼-inch strips
1½ cups sliced mushrooms (4 oz)
1 clove garlic, finely chopped
1 package (16 oz) fettuccine
½ cup grated Parmesan cheese

1 Mix tequila, limeade and lime peel in medium glass or plastic bowl. Stir in chicken. Cover and refrigerate 30 minutes.

2 Place chicken and marinade in 12-inch skillet. Stir in bell pepper, mushrooms and garlic. Cook over medium-high heat 10 to 12 minutes, stirring occasionally, until chicken is no longer pink in center.

3 Cook and drain fettuccine as directed on package. Divide fettuccine among 6 serving plates. Spoon chicken mixture over fettuccine. Sprinkle with cheese. Garnish with grated lime peel if desired.

1 Serving: Calories 375 (Calories from Fat 65); Total Fat 7g (Saturated Fat 3g); Cholesterol 115mg; Sodium 180mg; Total Carbohydrate 52g (Dietary Fiber 4g); Protein 30g

Lemon-Basil Chicken and Vegetables

Prep Time: 30 min ■ Start to Finish: 30min ■ 4 Servings

1 cup uncooked brown rice
1 lb boneless skinless chicken breasts
¼ teaspoon coarsely ground pepper
¼ teaspoon garlic powder
1 medium onion, cut into thin wedges
1 bag (1 lb) frozen baby bean and carrot blend (or other combination)
¾ cup water
½ cup lemon basil stir-fry sauce
1 teaspoon cornstarch

1 Cook rice as directed on package. While rice is cooking, cut chicken into 2x¼-inch strips. Spray 12-inch nonstick skillet with cooking spray; heat over medium-high heat. Add chicken to skillet; sprinkle with pepper and garlic powder. Stir-fry 4 to 6 minutes or until brown. Add onion; stir-fry 2 minutes.

2 Stir in frozen vegetables and water. Heat to boiling; reduce heat to medium. Cover and cook 5 to 6 minutes, stirring occasionally, until vegetables are tender.

3 Mix stir-fry sauce and cornstarch until smooth; stir into mixture in skillet. Heat to boiling, stirring constantly. Boil and stir 1 minute. Divide rice among bowls. Top with chicken mixture.

1 serving: Calories 410 (Calories from Fat 65); Total Fat 7g (Saturated Fat 2g); Cholesterol 70mg; Sodium 630mg; Total Carbohydrate 61g (Dietary Fiber 8g); Protein 33g

Thai-Style Coconut Chicken

Prep Time: 35 min ■ Start to Finish: 35 min ■ 4 Servings

1 tablespoon vegetable oil
1 lb boneless skinless chicken breasts, cut into bite-size pieces
1 teaspoon grated lime peel
1 teaspoon grated gingerroot
1 clove garlic, finely chopped
2 fresh serrano chiles or 1 jalapeño chile, seeded and finely chopped
1/4 cup finely chopped fresh cilantro
1 can (about 14 oz) coconut milk (not cream of coconut)

1 teaspoon packed brown sugar
1/2 teaspoon salt
1 tablespoon soy sauce
1 cup sugar snap pea pods
1 medium green bell pepper, cut into 1-inch cubes
1 medium tomato, chopped (3/4 cup)
1 tablespoon chopped fresh basil leaves
Hot cooked jasmine rice, if desired

1 In nonstick wok or 12-inch nonstick skillet, heat oil over high heat. Add chicken; stir-fry 2 to 3 minutes or until chicken is no longer pink in center. Add lime peel, gingerroot, garlic, chiles and cilantro; stir-fry 1 minute.

2 Pour coconut milk over chicken. Stir in brown sugar, salt, soy sauce, pea pods and bell pepper. Reduce heat to medium. Simmer uncovered 3 to 5 minutes, stirring occasionally, until vegetables are crisp-tender. Stir into tomato.

3 Spoon into shallow serving bowls; top with basil. Serve with rice.

1 Serving: Calories 430 (Calories from Fat 230); Total Fat 26g (Saturated Fat 17g); Cholesterol 85mg; Sodium 650mg; Total Carbohydrate 14g (Dietary Fiber 4g); Protein 35g

Typical of many Thai dishes, the consistency of this recipe is like a broth, yet it's full of flavor. If you prefer your Thai food quite hot, increase the number of chiles.

Pineapple-Glazed Spicy Chicken Breasts

Prep Time: 15 min ■ Start to Finish: 40 min ■ 4 Servings

Chicken

2 tablespoons packed dark brown
    sugar

1$^1/_2$ teaspoons salt

1$^1/_2$ teaspoons ground coriander

1$^1/_2$ teaspoons ground allspice

$^2/_3$ teaspoon ground cinnamon

$^1/_2$ teaspoon ground cumin

$^1/_4$ teaspoon ground red pepper
    (cayenne)

4 boneless skinless chicken breasts,
    pounded between pieces of
    waxed paper to $^1/_4$-inch thickness

2 tablespoons vegetable oil

Glaze

$^1/_2$ cup pineapple juice

$^1/_4$ cup real maple syrup

1 tablespoon lemon juice

2 tablespoons butter

2 teaspoons Dijon mustard

1 In 9-inch pie plate, mix brown sugar, salt, coriander, allspice, cinnamon, cumin and red pepper. Rub chicken with oil, then coat all over with the spice mixture.

2 In 1-quart saucepan, heat all glaze ingredients to boiling over medium heat. Cook uncovered about 10 minutes, stirring occasionally, until thickened and syrupy and reduced to $^1/_2$ cup. Remove from heat. Remove 2 tablespoons glaze to brush over chicken.

3 Spray grill rack with cooking spray or brush with oil. Heat coals or gas grill for medium-high heat. Grill chicken uncovered 4 to 5 minutes per side or until juice of chicken is clear when center of thickest part is cut.

4 When chicken is almost cooked through, brush with the reserved 2 tablespoons glaze. Grill 1 minute longer. Remove chicken from grill and drizzle with the remaining glaze.

1 Serving: Calories 370 (Calories from Fat 150); Total Fat 17g (Saturated Fat 5g); Cholesterol 90mg; Sodium 1060mg; Total Carbohydrate 26g (Dietary Fiber 0g); Protein 27g

Caramelized-Garlic Chicken

Prep Time: 30 min ▪ Start to Finish: 30 min ▪ 5 Servings

4 cloves garlic, finely chopped
1 tablespoon canola oil or butter
2 teaspoons packed brown sugar
$1/4$ teaspoon salt
1 lb boneless skinless chicken breast halves
$1/4$ cup water
4 slices tomato
4 oz Havarti or Swiss cheese, cut into $1/8$-inch slices
1 tablespoon chopped fresh or $1/2$ teaspoon dried basil leaves

1 Cook garlic and oil in 10-inch nonstick skillet over medium-low heat 1 to 2 minutes, stirring constantly, just until garlic begins to turn brown. Stir in brown sugar until melted.

2 Sprinkle salt over chicken. Add chicken to skillet. Cook 3 to 5 minutes, turning once, until brown. Add water. Cook over medium heat 8 to 10 minutes, turning once, until chicken is glazed and no longer pink when centers of thickest pieces are cut and liquid has evaporated. Chicken will be golden brown. Watch carefully to prevent scorching.

3 Top each chicken piece with tomato, cheese and basil. Cover and heat 1 to 2 minutes or until cheese is melted.

1 Serving: Calories 240 (Calories from Fat 145); Total Fat 13g (Saturated Fat 7g); Cholesterol 90mg; Sodium 330mg; Total Carbohydrate 4g (Dietary Fiber 0g); Protein 27g

Dijon Chicken Smothered in Mushrooms

Prep Time: 22 min ▪ Start to Finish: 22 min ▪ 4 Servings

4 boneless skinless chicken breast halves (about 1 lb)
1/4 cup all-purpose flour
1/2 teaspoon salt
1/4 teaspoon pepper
2 tablespoons olive or canola oil
1/2 cup roasted garlic-seasoned chicken broth (from 14-oz can)
1 1/2 tablespoons Dijon mustard
1 jar (4 1/2 oz) sliced mushrooms, drained
Chopped fresh thyme, if desired

1 If using pork, cut into 1-inch-thick slices. Place chicken between 2 sheets of plastic wrap or waxed paper. Flatten chicken to 1/4-inch thickness with meat mallet or rolling pin. Mix flour, salt and pepper in shallow dish.

2 Heat oil in 12-inch nonstick skillet over medium-high heat. Coat both sides of chicken with flour mixture. Cook chicken in hot oil 6 to 8 minutes, turning once, until chicken is no longer pink in center. Remove chicken to serving plate; cover to keep warm.

3 Stir broth into skillet. Heat to boiling over medium-high heat. Stir in mustard and mushrooms. Cook 2 to 3 minutes, stirring frequently, until slightly thickened. Spoon sauce over chicken. Sprinkle with thyme.

1 Serving: Calories 210 (Calories from Fat 60); Total Fat 7g (Saturated Fat 1.5g); Cholesterol 70mg; Sodium 630mg; Total Carbohydrate 9g (Dietary Fiber 0g); Protein 28g

Chicken Marsala

Prep Time: 45 min ■ Start to Finish: 45 min ■ 4 Servings

$1/4$ cup all-purpose flour
$1/4$ teaspoon salt
$1/4$ teaspoon pepper
4 boneless skinless chicken breast halves (about $1^{1}/_4$ lb)
2 tablespoons olive or vegetable oil
2 cloves garlic, finely chopped
1 cup sliced mushrooms (3 lb)
$1/4$ cup chopped fresh parsley or 1 tablespoon parsley flakes
$1/2$ cup dry Marsala wine or chicken broth

1 Mix flour, salt and pepper. Coat chicken with flour mixture; shake off excess flour.

2 Heat oil in 10-inch skillet over medium-high heat. Cook garlic, mushrooms and parsley in oil 5 minutes, stirring frequently.

3 Add chicken to skillet. Cook uncovered about 8 minutes, turning once, until chicken is brown. Add wine. Cook uncovered 8 to 10 minutes, turning once, until chicken is no longer pink in center.

You can substitute dry sherry for the Marsala, if you like. Amber-hued Marsala wine comes from Sicily and tastes similar to sherry. Marsala can be either dry or sweet, the dry used for savory dishes and the sweet usually for desserts.

1 Serving: Calories 290 (Calories from Fat 100); Total Fat 11g (Saturated Fat 2g); Cholesterol 85mg; Sodium 230mg; Total Carbohydrate 11g (Dietary Fiber 1g); Protein 33g

6

grill it!

Flavor Boosters

Marinades, spice rubs and sauces are three terrific ways to add big flavors to chicken breasts and they couldn't be easier to use. Give the meat a quick rubdown with marinade or rub before cooking and let it sit and absorb the flavors, or slather cooked chicken with sauce. Supermarket shelves overflow with flavors ranging from sweet and tangy to hot and spicy, but it's almost as easy to whip up these recipes yourself.

Peppery Teriyaki Marinade

Prep Time: 10 min
Start to Finish: 10 min
About 1/2 cup marinade (enough to
   flavor 1 1/2 pounds chicken)

1/4 cup soy sauce
2 tablespoons water
1 tablespoon lemon juice
1 tablespoon vegetable oil
1 teaspoon packed brown sugar
1/4 teaspoon coarsely ground pepper
1 clove garlic, finely chopped

   Mix all ingredients.

Ginger-Lime Marinade

Prep Time: 10 min
Start to Finish: 10 min
About 1/3 cup

1/4 cup lime juice
2 tablespoons olive or vegetable oil
1 teaspoon finely chopped gingerroot
1/4 teaspoon salt
 Dash of ground red pepper
   (cayenne)
1 clove garlic, crushed

   Mix all ingredients.

Marinades can add flavor in as little as 15 minutes, but 1 to 2 hours is best (save time by marinating overnight, but don't marinate longer than 24 hours). To marinate chicken breasts, place uncooked meat and marinade in a nonmetal dish and cover tightly, or place in a heavy-duty plastic bag that can be tightly sealed. Store in the refrigerator, turning chicken once or twice so marinade can reach all surfaces. Then grill, broil or sauté (see pages 6–7). Marinade for raw meat is not reusable; discard any leftover marinade or boil at least one minute and use as a sauce.

Cajun Spice Rub

Prep Time: 5 min
Start to Finish: 5 min
About 1 tablespoon (enough for 1 lb meat)

1 teaspoon black pepper
1/2 teaspoon white pepper
1/2 teaspoon ground red pepper (cayenne)
1/2 teaspoon salt
1/2 teaspoon ground cumin
1/2 teaspoon ground nutmeg
1 tablespoon vegetable oil

1. In small bowl, mix all ingredients except oil.

2. To use, brush oil on both sides of 1 pound chicken breasts. Spread rub evenly on chicken. Cook as desired.

Spicy Texas Barbecue Sauce

Prep Time: 15 min
Start to Finish: 1 hr 15 min
About 5 cups sauce

1 cup ketchup
1/2 cup packed brown sugar
1/4 cup lime juice
2 to 3 tablespoons ground red chilies or chili powder
1 tablespoon vegetable oil
1 tablespoon Worcestershire sauce
3 medium onions, chopped (1 1/2 cups)
2 jalapeño chiles, seeded and finely chopped
2 cloves garlic, finely chopped
1 can (12 oz) tomato paste
1 can or bottle (12 oz) regular or nonalcoholic beer

1. In 2-quart saucepan, heat all ingredients to boiling; reduce heat to low. Cover and simmer 1 hour, stirring occasionally.

2. Serve warm sauce over grilled, broiled, or sautéed chicken breasts.

Capsaicin is the substance in chilies that makes them hot, hot, hot. You may want to wear plastic gloves when chopping chilies, as capsaicin can be irritating to your skin.

Barbecued Chicken Nachos

Prep Time: 10 min ■ Start to Finish: 20 min ■ 8 Servings

16 cups tortilla chips (about one 13.5-oz bag)
3 cups cut-up cooked chicken (about 1¹/₂ lb)
1¹/₃ cups barbecue sauce
2 cans (15 oz each) chili beans in sauce, undrained
2 cans (2¹/₄ oz each) sliced ripe olives, drained
2 large tomatoes, chopped (2 cups)
6 cups shredded Colby–Monterey Jack cheese blend (24 oz)

1 Heat coals or gas grill for direct heat. Spray two 30×18-inch pieces of heavy-duty aluminum foil with cooking spray.

2 Spread tortilla chips on centers of foil pieces. Mix chicken and barbecue sauce. Spoon chili beans, chicken mixture, olives, tomatoes and cheese on chips.

3 Wrap foil securely around tortilla chips. Cover and grill foil packets, seam sides up, 4 to 6 inches from medium heat 8 to 10 minutes or until cheese is melted.

Chips on the grill? Trust us—it's great!

1 Serving: Calories 410 (Calories from Fat 235); Total Fat 23g (Saturated Fat 10g); Cholesterol 65mg; Sodium 1110mg; Total Carbohydrate 33g (Dietary Fiber 4g); Protein 23g

Orange-Tarragon Chicken

Prep Time: 37 min ▪ Start to Finish: 8 hrs 37 min ▪ 4 Servings

Orange-Tarragon Marinade
2 teaspoons grated orange peel
$1/2$ cup orange juice
$1/4$ cup vegetable oil
$1/4$ cup white wine vinegar
2 tablespoons chopped shallots
1 teaspoon dried tarragon leaves
$1/2$ teaspoon salt

Chicken
4 boneless skinless chicken breast halves (about $1^1/4$ lb)
Chopped tomato, if desired
Chopped fresh tarragon leaves, if desired

1 In shallow glass or plastic dish, mix all marinade ingredients. Add chicken; turn to coat. Cover dish and refrigerate at least 8 hours but no longer than 24 hours.

2 Brush grill rack with vegetable oil. Heat coals or gas grill for direct heat. Remove chicken from marinade; reserve marinade.

3 Cover and grill chicken, skin sides up, over medium heat 15 to 20 minutes, turning once and brushing with marinade, until juice of chicken is no longer pink when centers of thickest pieces are cut.

4 In 1-quart saucepan, heat remaining marinade to boiling; boil and stir 1 minute. Serve with chicken. Garnish with tomato and tarragon.

1 Serving: Calories 315 (Calories from Fat 190); Total Fat 21g (Saturated Fat 4g); Cholesterol 75mg; Sodium 360mg; Total Carbohydrate 4g (Dietary Fiber 0g); Protein 27g

Grilled Margarita Chicken Salad

Prep Time: 35 min ■ Start to Finish: 35 min ■ 4 Servings

1/2 cup frozen (thawed) nonalcoholic margarita mix
1/4 cup olive or vegetable oil
2 tablespoons white wine vinegar
4 boneless skinless chicken breasts (1 1/4 lb)
6 cups bite-size pieces assorted salad greens
1 cup sliced strawberries
1 medium mango, peeled, pitted and sliced
1 medium avocado, peeled, pitted and sliced
1/4 cup chopped fresh cilantro

1 Heat coals or gas grill for direct heat. To make dressing, in small bowl, stir margarita mix, oil and vinegar with wire whisk until well blended. Measure 1/4 cup dressing for basting chicken; reserve remaining dressing for serving.

2 Cover and grill chicken over medium heat 15 to 20 minutes, turning and brushing occasionally with 1/4 cup dressing, until juice of chicken is no longer pink when centers of thickest pieces are cut.

3 Cut chicken into slices. In large bowl, toss salad greens, chicken and strawberries; divide among 4 plates. Arrange mango and avocado around each salad. Sprinkle with cilantro. Drizzle with reserved dressing.

1 Serving: Calories 460 (Calories from Fat 225); Total Fat 25g (Saturated Fat 4g); Cholesterol 75mg; Sodium 90mg; Total Carbohydrate 35g (Dietary Fiber 6g); Protein 29g

Grilled Chicken Citrus Salad

Prep Time: 30 min ▪ Start to Finish: 30 min ▪ 4 Servings

$^2/_3$ cup citrus vinaigrette dressing
4 boneless skinless chicken breasts (about $1^1/_4$ lb)
1 bag (10 oz) ready-to-eat romaine lettuce
2 unpeeled apples, cubed (about 2 cups)
$^1/_2$ cup coarsely chopped dried apricots
2 medium green onions, sliced (2 tablespoons)
$^1/_2$ cup chopped honey-roasted peanuts

1 Heat gas or charcoal grill. Place 2 tablespoons of the dressing in small bowl. Brush all sides of chicken with the 2 tablespoons dressing.

2 In large bowl, toss lettuce, apples, apricots and onions; set aside.

3 Place chicken on grill. Cover grill; cook over medium heat 8 to 10 minutes, turning once, until juice of chicken is clear when center of thickest part is cut.

4 Add remaining dressing to lettuce mixture; toss. On 4 plates, divide lettuce mixture. Cut chicken crosswise to slices; place on lettuce. Sprinkle with peanuts.

There are so many enticing prewashed salad greens available—feel free to use your favorite for this recipe.

1 Serving: Calories 550 (Calories from Fat 280); Total Fat 31g (Saturated Fat 4g); Cholesterol 90mg; Sodium 510mg; Total Carbohydrate 30g (Dietary Fiber 6g); Protein 39g

Grilled Chicken Satay Salad

Prep Time: 35 min ▪ Start to Finish: 1 hr 35 min ▪ 6 Servings

Salad

1 flour tortilla (8 inch), cut in half, then
    cut crosswise into $1/8$- to $1/4$- inch
    strips
4 boneless, skinless chicken breast
    halves (about $1^1/4$ lb)
6 cups bite-size pieces mixed salad
    greens
1 cup finely shredded red cabbage
$1/3$ cup shredded carrot
$1/4$ cup chopped fresh cilantro or parsley

Peanut Satay Dressing

$1/3$ cup rice vinegar or cider vinegar
$1/4$ cup creamy peanut butter
3 tablespoons finely chopped peanuts
2 tablespoons sugar
2 tablespoons vegetable oil
2 tablespoons sesame oil
1 tablespoon soy sauce
$1/2$ teaspoon finely chopped
    gingerroot
1 clove garlic, finely chopped

1 Heat oven to 350°F. Arrange tortilla strips in single layer on ungreased cookie sheet. Bake 7 to 11 minutes or until lightly browned.

2 Meanwhile, make dressing by beating all ingredients in small bowl with wire whisk until smooth and creamy. Place chicken in resealable plastic food-storage bag; add 3 tablespoons of the dressing. Seal bag; turn to coat chicken. Refrigerate 1 to 2 hours. Refrigerate remaining dressing. Toss remaining ingredients in large bowl; cover and refrigerate.

3 Brush grill rack with vegetable oil. Heat coals or gas grill for direct heat. Cover and grill chicken 4 to 6 inches from medium heat 10 to 15 minutes, turning once, until juice of chicken is no longer pink when centers of thickest pieces are cut.

4 Cut chicken into strips. Add chicken and remaining dressing to salad; toss. Divide salad among 6 plates. Sprinkle with tortilla strips.

About 3/4 cup purchased peanut dressing can be substituted
    for the Peanut Satay Dressing.

1 Serving: Calories 335 (Calories from Fat 180); Total Fat 20g (Saturated Fat 4g); Cholesterol 50mg; Sodium 320mg; Total Carbohydrate 15g (Dietary Fiber 3g); Protein 24g

Caribbean Chicken Kabobs

Prep Time: 35 min ■ Start to Finish: 35 min ■ 8 Servings

1²/₃ lb boneless skinless chicken breast halves, cut into 1¹/₂-inch pieces
¹/₄ cup vegetable oil
3 tablespoons Caribbean jerk seasoning (dry)
1 small pineapple, rind removed and pineapple cut into 1-inch cubes
1 medium red bell pepper, cut into 1-inch pieces
1 small red onion, cut into 1-inch pieces

1 Brush grill rack with vegetable oil. Heat coals or gas grill for direct heat.

2 Brush chicken with 2 tablespoons of the oil. Place chicken and jerk seasoning in resealable plastic food-storage bag. Shake bag to coat chicken with seasoning. Thread chicken, pineapple, bell pepper and onion alternately on each of eight 12-inch metal skewers, leaving ¹/₄-inch space between each piece. Brush kabobs with remaining 2 tablespoons oil.

3 Cover and grill kabobs over medium heat 15 to 20 minutes, turning once, until chicken is no longer pink in center.

Juicy fresh pineapple chunks and jerk seasoning turn this chicken dinner into a taste of the tropics. Why not mix up a big pitcher of lemonade as well?

1 Serving: Calories 210 (Calories from Fat 90); Total Fat 10g (Saturated Fat 2g); Cholesterol 60mg; Sodium 210mg; Total Carbohydrate 8g (Dietary Fiber 1g); Protein 22g

Paella on the Grill

Prep Time: 45 min ▪ Start to Finish: 1 hr 45 min ▪ 6 Servings

Saffron Marinade
1 cup chicken broth
½ cup sherry wine vinegar
½ teaspoon salt
¼ teaspoon curry powder
¼ teaspoon crushed saffron threads or ground turmeric
2 cloves garlic, finely chopped

Paella
1 lb boneless skinless chicken breasts, cut into 1-inch pieces
1 lb uncooked medium shrimp in shells
½ lb chorizo sausage, cut into 1-inch pieces
8 plum (Roma) tomatoes, cut into fourths
1 can (about 14 oz) artichoke hearts, drained and cut in half
1 cup pitted kalamata or Greek olives
Hot cooked rice, if desired

1 Mix all Saffron Marinade ingredients. In glass or plastic dish or resealable food-storage plastic bag, place all Paella ingredients except rice. Pour marinade over mixture; stir to coat. Cover dish or seal bag and refrigerate 1 hour.

2 Heat coals or gas grill for direct heat. Remove chicken mixture from marinade; reserve marinade. Place chicken mixture in grill basket.

3 Cover and grill chicken mixture 4 inches from medium heat 20 to 25 minutes, stirring and brushing with marinade occasionally, until chicken is no longer pink in center. Discard any remaining marinade. Serve chicken mixture with rice.

1 Serving: Calories 365 (Calories from Fat 180); Total Fat 20g (Saturated Fat 7g); Cholesterol 150mg; Sodium 1260mg; Total Carbohydrate 14g (Dietary Fiber 5g); Protein 37g

Provolone-Smothered Chicken

Prep Time: 25 min ▪ Start to Finish: 55 min ▪ 4 Servings

4 boneless skinless chicken breast halves (about 1¹/₄ lb)
¹/₂ cup zesty Italian dressing
¹/₂ teaspoon garlic pepper blend
2 tablespoons chopped fresh basil leaves
4 thin slices tomato
4 slices (¹/₂ to ²/₃ oz each) provolone cheese

1 Place chicken in shallow dish. Pour dressing over chicken. Cover and refrigerate about 30 minutes.

2 Heat closed medium-size contact grill for 5 minutes. Remove chicken from marinade; reserve marinade. Sprinkle chicken with garlic pepper. Place chicken on grill. Close grill. Grill 4 to 6 minutes, brushing with marinade once, until juice of chicken is no longer pink when centers of thickest pieces are cut. Discard remaining marinade.

3 Sprinkle each chicken breast with basil; top with tomato and cheese. Let stand on grill 3 to 5 minutes or until cheese is melted.

1 Serving: Calories 250 (Calories from Fat 100); Total Fat 11g (Saturated Fat 4g); Cholesterol 95mg; Sodium 270mg; Total Carbohydrate 2g (Dietary Fiber 0g); Protein 35g

Grilled Pesto Chicken Packets

Prep Time: 15 min ▪ Start to Finish: 40 min ▪ 4 Servings

4 boneless skinless chicken breast halves (1¹/₄ lb)
8 plum (Roma) tomatoes, cut into ¹/₂ inch slices
4 small zucchini, cut into ¹/₂-inch slices
¹/₂ cup basil pesto

1 Heat coals or gas grill for direct heat. Place 1 chicken breast half, 2 sliced tomatoes and 1 sliced zucchini on one side of four 18×12-inch sheets of heavy-duty aluminum foil. Spoon 2 tablespoons pesto over chicken mixture on each sheet.

2 Fold foil over chicken and vegetables so edges meet. Seal edges, making tight ¹/₂-inch fold; fold again. Allow space on sides for circulation and expansion.

3 Cover and grill packets 4 to 5 inches from medium heat 20 to 25 minutes or until juice of chicken is no longer pink when centers of thickest pieces are cut. Place packets on plates. Cut large X across top of packet; fold back foil.

1 Serving: Calories 330 (Calories from Fat 180); Total Fat 20g (Saturated Fat 4g); Cholesterol 80mg; Sodium 350mg; Total Carbohydrate 10g (Dietary Fiber 3g); Protein 31g

Helpful Nutrition and Cooking Information

Recommended intake for a daily diet of 2,000 calories as set by the Food and Drug Administration

Total Fat	Less than 65g
Saturated Fat	Less than 20g
Cholesterol	Less than 300mg
Sodium	Less than 2,400mg
Total Carbohydrate	300g
Dietary Fiber	25g

Calculating Nutrition Information

- The first ingredient is used wherever a choice is given (such as ⅓ cup sour cream or plain yogurt).

- The first ingredient amount is used wherever a range is given (such as 2 to 3 teaspoons).

- The first serving number was used wherever a range is given (such as 4 to 6 servings).

- "If desired" ingredients and recipe variations were not included (such as sprinkle with brown sugar, if desired).

- Only the amount of a marinade or frying oil that is absorbed by the food during preparation was calculated.

Ingredients Used in Recipe Testing and Nutrition Calculations

The following ingredients, based on most commonly purchased ingredients, are used unless indicated otherwise:

- large eggs, 2% milk, 80%-lean ground beef, canned chicken broth and vegetable oil spread containing at least 65% fat when margarine is used.

- Solid vegetable shortening (not butter, margarine, or nonstick cooking spray) is used to grease pans.

Equipment Used in Recipe Testing

- Cookware and bakeware without nonstick coatings were used, unless otherwise indicated.

- No dark-colored, black or insulated bakeware was used.

- When a pan is specified, a metal pan was used; a baking dish or pie plate means ovenproof glass was used.

- An electric hand mixer was used for mixing when mixer speeds are specified.

Metric Conversion Guide

VOLUME

U.S. Units	Canadian Metric	Australian Metric
¼ teaspoon	1 mL	1 ml
½ teaspoon	2 mL	2 ml
1 teaspoon	5 mL	5 ml
1 tablespoon	15 mL	20 ml
¼ cup	50 mL	60 ml
⅓ cup	75 mL	80 ml
½ cup	125 mL	125 ml
⅔ cup	150 mL	170 ml
¾ cup	175 mL	190 ml
1 cup	250 mL	250 ml
1 quart	1 liter	1 liter
1½ quarts	1.5 liters	1.5 liters
2 quarts	2 liters	2 liters
2½ quarts	2.5 liters	2.5 liters
3 quarts	3 liters	3 liters
4 quarts	4 liters	4 liters

WEIGHT

U.S. Units	Canadian Metric	Australian Metric
1 ounce	30 grams	30 grams
2 ounces	55 grams	60 grams
3 ounces	85 grams	90 grams
4 ounces (¼ pound)	115 grams	125 grams
8 ounces (½ pound)	225 grams	225 grams
16 ounces (1 pound)	455 grams	500 grams
1 pound	455 grams	½ kilogram

MEASUREMENTS

Inches	Centimeters
1	2.5
2	5.0
3	7.5
4	10.0
5	12.5
6	15.0
7	17.5
8	20.5
9	23.0
10	25.5
11	28.0
12	30.5
13	33.0

TEMPERATURES

Fahrenheit	Celsius
32°	0°
212°	100°
250°	120°
275°	140°
300°	150°
325°	160°
350°	180°
375°	190°
400°	200°
425°	220°
450°	230°
475°	240°
500°	260°

NOTE: The recipes in this cookbook have not been developed or tested using metric measures. When converting recipes to metric, some variations in quality may be noted.

Index

Page numbers in italics indicate illustrations.

Whatever's on the menu, make it easy with *Betty Crocker*

Betty Crocker
chicken
tonight
100 Recipes for the Way You Really Cook

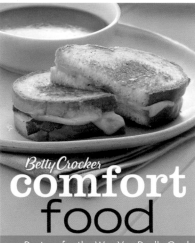

Betty Crocker
comfort
food
100 Recipes for the Way You Really Cook

Betty Crocker
party
food
100 Recipes for the Way You Really Cook

Betty Crocker
quick
fixes
100 Recipes for the Way You Really Cook